Ancient Mines of Kitchi-Gummi

Cypriot/Minoan Traders
in
North America

By

Roger L. Jewell

Edit, layout and cover design
by
Mary E Jewell

Published by
Jewell Histories
Fairfield, PA

Third Edition
2011

Printed in the United States of America
by

Hagerstown Bookbinding and Printing

ISBN # 978-0-9678413-2-8

Library of Congress Catalog Card Number

To order contact
jewellhistories.com
or
Jewell Histories
15 Trout Run Trail
Fairfield, PA
17320

(717) 642-8342

Acknowledgments

There are numerous individuals who are waging the battle for a more accurate ancient American history. Far too many individuals to name here; however, there are three organizations in which many of them work.

The first group I came in touch with was ISAC, The Institute for the Study of American Cultures. This group, based in Georgia, also had a small Midwestern Chapter. They deserve much credit for the work they are doing, collecting and cataloging evidence of this subject.

The second group, NEARA (The New England Antiquities Research Association) is based in New England. Individuals in this group are working tirelessly to study and protect the monolithic stonework in their area. They have been very helpful in providing a critique on the first edition of this book and they also provide a substantial amount of the information for this expanded second edition.

The third group, The Louisiana Mound Society, sadly is no longer active. For years, they provided an informative newsletter on the subject. All of these groups were very helpful in providing information for my edification and study.

I am especially thankful for the assistance of NEARA members. James Guthrie for all the material he has provided initially and the continuing work he has done on the language issue. I am also grateful to Martin Breck who directed me to two wonderful stone chambers in Putnam County, New York. Judy Butler, of the Vermont chapter, for the copper mine tour that lead to my understanding of the role of pigments and dyes in ancient New England history. I much appreciate the feedback on my book from Joan Lambert, Morris Payne, and Bob Stone and their discussions on the early water levels in respect to American Stonehenge.

Mary Linderoth, Dennis Dougherty and Fred Rydholm, of Upper Michigan, were of great help from the very beginning. Without their information and support the book may not have been written.

Last, I would like to thank my family, my four daughters who assisted on the first edition, and my wife, Mary, who has struggled to make my English readable and the layout understandable in this second edition. I'm sure those who have read the first edition will be pleased with the changes.

Many thanks to all of you

Roger & Dad

Foreword

There have been several books written about the tremendous amounts of pure copper that had been set free by the glacier in Michigan's Upper Peninsula and Isle Royal, and undeniable proof of the mining and gathering of that copper in the distant past. Also, there have been several authors who have speculated on how much copper was removed in ancient times. Some have flatly stated that whatever the amount, some of it had to have gone elsewhere as there seems to be no end (destination) of a copper trade on this continent.

But Roger Jewell has gone far beyond these subjects to present a compelling case for one special ethnic group that took part in that trade for 1200 years. He has provided dates and historical circumstances, which seem to fit these people as the carriers of Lake Superior copper to the Mediterranean.

Thirty years ago, this book would have been openly ridiculed by archaeologists and pre-historians. For a hundred years, it has been the position of the American establishment that America was completely isolated and that no one crossed the great oceans before Columbus.

In the last half of this century, there have been some great revelations by people such as Thor Hyerdhal, Barry Fell, Henrietta Mertz, Joseph Mahan, and Gunnar Thompson, to name a few, all who have presented much proof that people have been coming to America for thousands of years. These oceans were not barriers as was once thought, but were highways.

It is significant that one of the great pieces of evidence lies in the solving of the ancient puzzle of the mysterious copper trade that has been suggested by so many.

Roger Jewell has been collecting this evidence for many years and here in a readable and understandable form is the story of one group of copper traders.

The American public has never been very familiar with ancient European and African history, nor even with ancient American history. They have learned well European history—the history of Europeans in America starting with Columbus.

Now in the early years of the new millennium, Mr. Jewell's book will stand as one of the first signs of the new awakening. To be sure many more will follow. The authorities who have been frustrated by strange finds for years, but were unable to write them up because of their preconceived ideas and the popular dogma among their colleagues, will now be free to express their views in a scientific manner. Nothing is a fake until it is absolutely proven to be a fake. All the pieces of the puzzle must be studied and put on the table. The fakes won't fit when the puzzle is completed.

This work is one of the first pieces to this worldwide puzzle. It is an early step in finding out the origins of the American Indians, and where their hundreds of tribes and languages derived from.

It is an exciting time to be alive, just to observe how this great change in attitude will be dealt with. Will it come suddenly, like wildfire, or will academia try to stamp it out as they have in the past—but truth will out.

The professionals will have to start all over to catch up to Roger Jewell and other amateurs like him. Then we can all learn together and there will be a great surge of interest in ancient American archaeology and discovery. The *Ancient Mines of Kitchi-Gummi* is one of the early steps in that great discovery.

C. Fred Rydholm (Upper Michigan, Author & Historian)

Introduction

For the last 500 years, since Columbus *"discovered"* the New World, controversy has raged. Was he the first? Numerous books have been written about evidence that indicates otherwise. Were there others? Yes, now we know there were. Recently, the finding of Viking foundations in Canada has broken the myth, but some believe there were more, many more.

Was there sustained travel and trade between Europe and North America, back at the dawn of history, 4500 years ago? How did the peopling of the Americas really happen? In this controversy, the ancient copper mines of Lake Superior become an undeniable piece of evidence that there was trade.

This book weighs in on this controversy. It does this in a straightforward fashion. A simple case study of how these ancient mines came into existence, and the repercussions of the answer, are examined.

Many of you, local history buffs, students of ancient American history, anthropology, archaeology, and Native American studies, may never have heard of the ancient copper mines on Lake Superior. But for those who do know of them, the question was always there. Who dug approximately 5,000 copper mines 4500 years ago on Lake Superior's Isle Royale and adjoining areas? Why did they do it, and where is the copper now? How could 20 to 50 million pounds of copper be removed from this area in such a fashion, that it literally seems to have vanished? In this study, I have used three points of logic:

- First, no culture does an irrational act continuously for 1200 years.

- Second, in a study, if the theory is correct, it will explain all the pertinent evidence.

- Third, a correct solution will not be forthcoming, if the researcher ignores or destroys all the evidence he does not, at first, understand.

Keep these bits of logic in mind as you join me in this search for truth. We will provide the answer to who dug the ancient copper mines and why. When you are through, I think it will affect your understanding of ancient American history.

We all know knowledge is taught from one generation to the next. We also realize the older generation does not always appreciate it when these historical facts are questioned. Yet we all must understand, progress only comes when old, incomplete, or inadequate ideas are put aside in favor of new or more accurate information. Eventually, the student becomes the teacher, as cultures evolve.

This book is about the very process of truth. Open interaction between the teacher and the student is essential. This interaction must allow for new ideas and technologies to evolve in an environment of trust and cooperation, if education is to benefit.

For those of you who read the first edition, the second edition, and this third edition have several corrections and twenty-seven pages of new information. This new section describes the traders' involvement in New England and the Mississippi River Valley. The new DNA evidence is presented along with an interesting discussion of an ancient drug trade. This information has been presented in an epilog, since it is an expansion of ideas beyond the boundaries of the original manuscript.

Enjoy this book, for it is part of your Ancient North American History, a subject that is as yet, in my opinion, not being taught.

Note - Some ancient sound based words are spelled differently in different references. In the text the most common spelling will be used. In the quotes, the quoted authors spelling will be used.

Table of Contents

1 Description of The Mines

The copper mines on Lake Superior were first being mined over 4400 years ago. This is about 2000 years before the classical Greek period; we measure our civilization from or about 1200 years before the Boy Pharaoh Tutankhamen was buried in his famous gold mask.

Huge amounts of copper were removed. Conservative estimates are between 20 and 50 million pounds. This was done over a 1200-year period between 2400 and 1200 BC.

Who could have done it and why? Where is the copper? These and other questions have not yet been answered to the satisfaction of many of us. The professional answer falls short of a plausible explanation in many ways, most of which we will examine further here.

Early Volume Estimates and Copper Description

First, I want to point out some stories found in the early history of the area that will give an idea of how big this copper resource was.

There is much evidence of these native copper pits as they are called in the early literature. The early Jesuits were some of the first to speak about the copper at Lake Superior and the high religious esteem in which the Indians held it.

The following quote is typical of their comments.

> *One often finds at the bottom of the water (of Lake Superior) pieces of pure copper, often of ten to twenty livre's weight. (1 livre = 1.1 lb.) I have several times seen such pieces in the savage's hands; and, since they are superstitious, they keep them as so many divinities, or as presents which the Gods dwelling beneath the water have given them, and on which their welfare is to depend. For this reason they preserve these pieces of copper, wrapped, among their most precious possessions. Some have kept them for more than fifty years; others have had them in their family from time immemorial, and cherish them as household Gods . . . Jesuit Missionary, Claude Allouez. 1665. (5) p - 48*

Louis Cass and Henry Rowe, two other people we have heard much about, were well acquainted with the copper in Lake Superior. In 1820, Louis Cass, then governor of the Michigan territory, and Henry Rowe

Schoolcraft, mineralogist, undertook an expedition with one of its objectives to gather information about the copper deposits on the shores of Lake Superior. For anyone looking for copper, it was customary to visit the famous copper boulder located a few miles up the Ontonagon River. These men were all well acquainted with the old mines and the extensive float copper. In fact, it is safe to say that when the New Michigan Territory was mapped, the boundary was located way out in Lake Superior to include Isle Royal.

Although the mines and the copper assets are mentioned many times, much of the early writing was about the native "*superstitions*" concerning it. This was probably because the Jesuits saw their role as being those who needed to convert the "*savages.*"

Michigan State Report

In about 1850, the state of Michigan undertook the task of making a report. Although obviously exaggerated, this document points out that there were massive amounts of copper that existed on Lake Superior, and how easy it was to find. It was entitled "*Report on the Geology and Topography of a Portion of the Lake Superior Land District.*" There is an interesting quote of Father Dablon [1669-1670] on page 11 of Document Number 69.

> *Pushing along to Le Grand Anse, (Neepigon bay,) we came to an island called 'Thunder Island,' which is noted for its abundance of metal. (This is probably St. Ignace) Further to the west is an Island called Menong, (Isle Royale,) celebrated for its copper. It is large, being twenty-five leagues long and seven leagues distant from the mainland. One bay at the northeast extremity is particularly remarkable. It is bounded by steep cliffs of clay, in which there may be seen several strata or beds of red copper separated from each other by layers of earth. In the water is seen copper sand, which may be gathered with spoons, although there are pieces as large as acorns. This large Island is surrounded by several smaller ones, some of which are said to consist entirely of copper. One, especially, near the northeast corner, is within gunshot of the main island. Further off in that direction is one-called Manitou-minis, on account of the abundance of copper. It is said by those who have visited it, that on a stone being thrown against it, a sound like that of brass when struck is heard. (1) p – 11*

After having reached the extremity of the lake, there may be seen (one days journey) on the south shore, by the waters edge, a mass of copper weighing 600 or 700 lb., so hard that steel cannot cut it but when heated it may be cut like lead. (1) p – 11

(Author's note: probably the Ontonagon Boulder) He goes on:

He bought of the savages a plate of pure copper two and one half feet square, weighing more than 100 lb. He supposes that they have been derived from Menong, . . . He mentions the fact that the Ottawa squaws, in digging holes in the sand to hide their corn, often find masses weighing 20 or 30 lb. (1) p - 11

Smithsonian Institute Report

The most thoughtful early writing on the mines comes from Charles Whittlesey, an investigator for the Smithsonian Institute. His paper was published in April 1862. Mr. Whittlesey apparently traveled to the mining district in the Houghton Peninsula of Michigan in the late 1850s or early 1860s. Whittlesey made many personal observations; however, what I consider equally as important is his reference to the miners' finds of the day. The commercial mining had been going on since about 1848 and had really gone into full swing in the 1850s. Consequently, there were about ten years worth of discoveries that were at his fingertips. These miners were not just passers-by they actually emptied the old pits, looking for the copper they often found sticking up out of the bottoms. It was very apparent to him that these ancient mines were dug with one objective in mind—that was to get copper—a lot of it. The only problem was they could not cut up the big pieces, for a few apparently too big to handle, were left. Of course, these were quickly removed by the more modern miners of the day.

In the Waterbury Mine, he describes the cedar shovels that were being used. They were shaped like ordinary paddles but were obviously used as shovels as indicated by the wear. In the Eagle Harbor Mine, he talks about the same type of shovels.

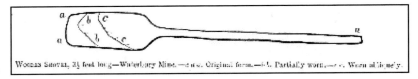

Wooden Shovel, 3½ feet long—Waterbury Mine.—a a a. Original form.—b b. Partially worn.—c c. Worn all the way.

G - 1 Shovel, (7) p - 8

Mr. Whittlesley describes how the ancient miners followed the ore veins. He mentions the Copper Falls vein, the East vein, the Hill vein and Owl Creek vein. The miners would normally work out the trap rock and copper as deep as they could. Then they would abandon the trench or hole and move on. The following copy of a sketch shows what they were finding.

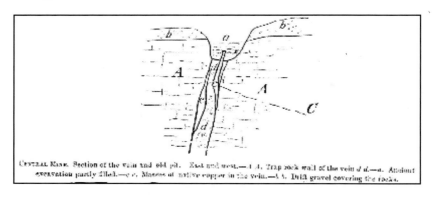

CENTRAL MINE. Section of the vein and old pit. East and west.—a a. Trap rock wall of the vein d d.—a. Ancient excavation partly filled.—c c. Masses of native copper in the vein.—b b. Drift gravel covering the rocks.

G - 2 Central Mine (7) p - 12

One personal quote is quite interesting:

In the autumn of 1851, Mr. Douglas informed me that there were indistinct signs of old works, half a mile from the lake on the northwest quarter of Section 1, T.53, and R.34, owned by the Isle Royal Mining Company. At the request of the directors of the company, a close reconnaissance of the ground was immediately made by myself. It required some assistance of the imagination to conceive that the slight and irregular depressions, which were dimly visible among the trees, were the works of men. Applying a compass to such of them as could be seen at one view, and carrying this line forward, it passed over or near the successive pits for a distance of one-third of a mile. We then set men to work to cut down a cross trench through one of them, and in a few hours reached the bottom. The vein and its walls were distinctly visible, having been worked out to a depth of ten feet, but the space was filled with rubbish nearly to the surface. Further examination, and cross trenching, disclosed the vein along a distance of three quarters of a mile, in places very broad with a bearing coincident to that of the formation.

It has now been worked to a depth of 250 feet, producing copper in rich masses, over a space twenty feet in thickness. In these wide places or pockets the early miners enlarged their pits to correspond, and carried their works to greater depths. (7) p 16

If this vein ran ¾ mile (3960 feet) and was an average of 10 feet deep and 5 feet thick or wide—just this one vein would have produced 198,000 cubic feet of ore. At 200 pounds per cubit foot and 3% richness, it would have produced 1.18 million pounds of copper or 590 tons. Already, the evidence of this was totally destroyed by the current miners of the day in 1862. The modern day miners, also working off the surface to some extent, probably destroyed hundreds of the best mines.

The Minnesota Mine was also discussed. It was here that a large piece of copper was discovered on a log crib:

Not far below the apparent bottom of a trough-like cavity where shaft No. one is now situated, among a mass of leaves, sticks, and water, Mr. Knapp discovered a detached mass of copper weighing nearly six tons. It lay upon a cob work of round logs or skids six to eight inches in diameter, the ends of which showed plainly the strokes of a small ax or cutting tool about 2 ½ inches wide. These marks were perfectly distinct . . . After several years, this vein has been found by the modern miners uncommonly rich and valuable for the size and number of its masses of copper. (7) p - 18

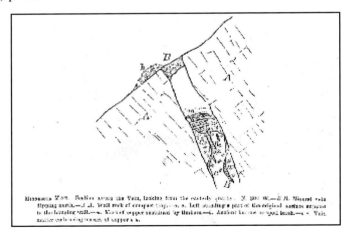

G - 3 Minnesota Mine (7) p - 17

These mines were on four veins that ran about two miles. The mineral range, of which they were a part, is about forty-five miles long. Copies of the sketched artifacts are included for your information.

Drier and DuTemple Description

The fact that there is a lot of copper on Lake Superior, in and of itself, is no real mystery. Approximately, 12 billion pounds have been taken out of the region by recent miners. In their book, *The Copper Mines Of Lake Superior,* Drier and DuTemple describe in detail these ancient mines. One of the most significant statements made by them is in reference to the amount of copper they estimate was removed from the mine.

In their book, it is stated that between 500 million pounds and 1.5 billion pounds of copper may have been removed from the Lake Superior basin. This was between 3000 and 5000 years ago. (More current estimates indicate this is probably quite high).

Mr. DuTemple clearly develops the scope of this early mining. It can best be stated in his own words:

> *It is estimated that 500 million pounds to perhaps more than one billion pounds of copper were mined prehistorically in the Lake Superior area. Where this copper went is still a mystery.*
>
> *Samples of charcoal taken from the bottom of two pits on Isle Royal in Lake Superior indicate that these pits were being worked at the bottom approximately 3500-4000 years ago. It is estimated that over 5000 of these pits occur around Lake Superior, most of them on the Keweenaw Peninsula. At this point one can only imagine what extensive investigation and cataloguing of information around these pits would do to clarify our understanding of these prehistoric peoples. (3) p - 15*

In the summers of 1953 and 1955 two of the mines near McCargo's Cove were cleaned out and carbon samples were taken:

> *The carbon samples taken from pieces of burnt logs at the bottom of the pit gave us the first definite indication that the mining was truly of prehistoric times, and at least 1000BC (3) p15*

Mr. DuTemple goes on to describe how the mining is done:

These miners built large bonfires on top of the copper-bearing vein in order to heat the rock. After the rock was thoroughly heated the fire was brushed away and cold water was immediately poured on the hot rock to fracture it. The pieces of copper bearing rock were then taken from the vein and broken by stone hammers in order to extricate the native copper which was imbedded therein."..."It also became more difficult as the pits became deeper. Pits over 30 feet deep have been found. These pits exist on Isle Royal on the Keweenaw Peninsula and on the Eastern end of Lake Superior above Ste. Marie's River. (3) p - 15

Mr. DuTemple presents some valuable information about copper in general around the world:

Native copper exist commercially only on the Keweenaw Peninsula. In the early 1920s another deposit of native copper was reported in Bolivia but it has not proved extensive enough to warrant economical mining operations. Native copper is also known to occur in small isolated pieces in the South Western United States ... (3) p - 16

Undoubtedly the easiest copper to obtain by prehistoric man was native copper. It seems reasonable that native copper would be used for perhaps thousands of years before the knowledge to refine the copper sulfide and copper oxide ore was known. The copper ores on the Sinai Peninsula in the Middle East and on Cyprus are copper sulfide ores. (3) p - 16

The copper is found in pure form in the Michigan deposits. Like many of the other much smaller deposits in the world, there is a particular kind of copper known as half-breed copper. These half-breed nuggets are pieces of pure copper with streaks or pockets of pure silver in them. This results in silver traces showing up in bronze, when it is made from pure copper instead of ores. This is important in tracing bronze back to its source mine:

The prehistoric miners around Lake Superior had some formidable problems of logistics in order to supply their workers . . . In spite of the large effort (perhaps as many as 10,000 men working for 1000 years it is believed that free men, and not slaves worked these pits

These people were undoubtedly good prospectors. Every mine that has been opened in the Lake Superior area is known to have been worked in prehistoric times. One can only imagine how long it took these people to locate these ore beds and to work them by the crude methods they used. The magnitude of the operation would indicate a strong metallurgic-ally oriented culture. There was undoubtedly a great economic demand to support this operation with men, material, food and transportation. Such effort was probably not put forth to secure copper for trinkets and ornamentals, but rather for working tools, probably for armaments, and to exchange in trade. (3) p - 16

Edwin J. Hulbert, the discoverer of the calumet conglomerate, reports four percent copper in the ore. Later stamping and sampling at the Albany Mine and Boston Mines showed 14.5 percent copper. (p 32 & 38)

If one assumes that an average pit is 20 feet in diameter and 30 feet deep, then it appears that something like 1000-1200 tons of ore were removed per pit. If the ore averaged five percent, or 100 pounds per ton then approximately 100,000 pounds of copper were removed per pit. If 5000 pits existed, as earlier estimates indicate (and all pits are copper bearing), then 100,000 pounds per pit in 5000 pits means that 500,000,000 pounds of copper were mined in prehistoric times—all of it without anything more than fire, stone hammers, and man power. If the ore sampled 15 percent, and if more than 5000 pits exist, then over 1.5 billion pounds of copper were mined. (3) p - 17

To some, this may seem a little dry and hard to grasp. But, for example, if this much copper was used to make armaments, and if each man's set weighed 50 pounds, the low estimate would equip 10 million soldiers.

Milwaukee Public Museum Report

To get a different view of the mines themselves, I would like to review the work of another writer on the subject, George E. West. In 1928. Mr. West was a Milwaukee attorney whose avocation was archaeology. He was also a member of the Board of Trustees of the Milwaukee Public Museum from 1906 to 1938. He took part in an expedition to Isle Royal in 1928 and his book, although not a real professional work by today's standards, he noted many items that will help the reader to understand the scope of these mines, and how they were viewed by anyone who really took the time to look at them.

Mr. West's book is entitled, *Copper: Its Mining and Use by the Aborigines of the Lake Superior Region:*

> *The expedition of the Milwaukee Public Museum in 1924 spent several days at McCargoe Cove for the purpose of studying the ancient mining operations that data might be secured for the construction of an environmental group for educational purposes. This group depicting an excavated pit of average size and showing the methods of aboriginal copper mining, is now on exhibition and has attracted much attention.*

> *While they were at the cove, a succession of pits and trenches were traced along the slope of the Amygdaloid ridge for nearly five miles with a width of about 400 yards thus covering an aggregate of one square mile. These pits when excavated are from four to ten feet deep and in some cases thirty feet across, usually cut into solid rock for a considerable distance." . . ."The number was estimated at fully ten thousand. In those excavated, much charcoal and many broken mauls were encountered, fifty-six being taken from a single pit. These and other observations clearly indicated that the primitive method of mining by the use of fire, water and pounding was employed. (2) p - 33*

Concerning the next few paragraphs, remember that the archaeologists doing this dig were not equipped with carbon dating, nor did they have a good pottery base for chronology. They stated:

> *The well-preserved condition of wooden implements found in the aboriginal pits caused early archaeologist to believe these mines to be of no great age. (2) p - 52*

> *Dr. Jacobson of Boston, who spent several years on Lake Superior during the early period of copper excitement, told Dr. Hoy in 1844, that: "The fresh condition of the wood-work, skids and ladders, and the fact that sharp axes were used in fitting the timber, is evidence that they were not of great antiquity. (2) p -52*

> *The writer, during his visit to the mining region on the south shore in 1875, saw a ladder, two paddles and fragments of a birch bark receptacle, taken from one of the ancient pits. These were all in a good state of preservation, excepting that the birch bark when dried was very brittle. This ladder . . . was cut off by hacking, with some instrument, clear around the portion to be cut and not cut from two sides, as a white man does. The instrument used was reasonably sharp and might have been a copper or stone ax. (2) p -52.*

We now know how really ancient these mines are. Their wooden tools became waterlogged and were submerged in the flooded mine pit for thousands of years. We will cover the time periods later in this section.

More Recent Volume Estimates and Descriptions

In the 1950s, Drier and DuTemple picked up on the carbon dated time problem. The massive number of mines was local common knowledge. The intellectuals also picked up on the timing problem. In the 1960s, there was a resurgence of interest in the mines. A paper was prepared named, *Lake Superior Copper and Indians* by J.B. Griffin, of the Anthropology Dept. of the University of Michigan in Ann Arbor. The man doing the work and running the survey crew was Tyler Bastian. Tyler also wrote his masters thesis on the subject in 1963 at the University of Utah, in Salt Lake City. This has been the only on-the-ground study concerning the volume of ore extracted to my knowledge.

Guthrie Investigations

I was recently told about a man who was about to publish a paper on the exact concept of how much ore may have been extracted by the native miners, and what percentage of it had been relocated. I made the contact and was delighted to learn about Dr. James L. Guthrie's paper entitled, *Great Lakes Copper - Still Missing*. Jim submitted his paper to the New *England Antiquities Research Association* for publication. It was published in an abbreviated form in the NEARA Journal, Volume XXX, No. 3 & 4, Winter/Spring 1996.

> *"The Mines of Isle Royal" - General Description,*
> *As described by Rapp et al.*
> *The famous Isle Royal and Keweenaw Peninsula native copper deposits are of three types: (1) Amygdaloidal lodes in basalt flow (2) Conglomerate lodes in intercalated sediments, and (3) lodes in fissure veins. The most important production (more than 90 percent of the ore) was from six ore horizons; one in a long conglomerate and five in the tops of lava flows. Rapp (1990:480-481)*
> *The deep fissure mines have caused the most comment, but contribute less than one percent of the volume. They are typically about four feet wide at the surface, pinching off at the bottom,*

which may be more than twenty feet below ground level. They occur along fractures and some times yield long sheets of tubular copper. (6) p - 60

During the summers of 1960, 1961, and 1962, survey led by Tyler Bastian spent 35 weeks locating and documenting the ancient mines (Bastian-1963). They located 36 fissure mines with typical volumes of about 200 cubic feet. Only nine had been excavated at the time. The largest was "pit 25" at the Minong site described by Drier (1961) and Bastian (1963:49-50). Its surface opening measured four feet by more than twenty feet, but it tapered to less than a foot and a half wide at a depth of 16 feet, making its volume about 800 cubic feet. A combination of silting and later mining prevented a complete listing of the ancient mines, but Bastion guessed (1963:49) that the total number of fissure mines on Isle Royal had been a hundred at most. The total volume of these, according to his, would have been about 20,000 cubic feet, or the equivalent of a dozen of the more important lode mines. A few fissure mines on the main land are known to have been at least 20 feet deep. The deepest one documented is a 26-foot pit in Ontonagon County, discovered by Samuel O. Knapp in 1848 (Foster and Whitney 1850:159).

The larger but shallower lode mines are in conglomerates and Amygdaloids that are only a few feet thick. Rapp, et al. describes the ore deposits as follows: (6) p - 60

Ores are found in the fragmented, brecciated tops of individual flows, in which rock was broken during consolidation and flow into jumbled masses of highly permeable angular fragments. Other ores are consolidated in simple scoriaceous flow tops, and a few occur in tops in which vesicles coalesced and formed longer connected passages. Flow tops are reddish because of the hematite formed by oxidation during the solidification of the Basalt... conglomerates lodes or deposits in sediments occur as cement in reddish felsite conglomerate beds or lenses, 3-7 (meters; i.e., 10-23 feet) thick. (Rapp et al. 1990:481)

The lode mines account for more than 99% of the pit volume on Isle Royal. They are typically 15-20 feet in diameter and six or seven feet deep. (6) p - 60

Bastian recorded 1015 lode mines on Isle Royal (p-31), but he thought there might have been as many as 2000 originally (p-31). This does not include innumerable 'potholes' that are too small or covered over to be noticed by any one but the most experienced explorers. Only five pits had been excavated at the time of

Bastian's survey. He reports that the largest one adequately recorded was 'pit 54' (p-30). Bastian conducted a partial re-excavation of pit-54, finding it to be 15 feet wide and 30 feet long, with a depth from five to nine feet. This indicates a volume on the order 3000 cubic feet, apparently near the upper limit. (6) P- 60

Bastian estimated the average volume of the Isle Royal lode mines to be 1500 cubic feet; about a sixth of that estimated by DuTemple. (6) p - 60

If there were 10,000 mines on Isle Royal as claimed by Gillman and by Barrett, a reasonable distribution by size is 2000 lode mines averaging 1500 cubic feet (3,000,000 cubic feet total) 8,000 potholes of about 4 cubic feet (32,000 cubic feet, and 100 fissures (20,000 cubic feet). In this simplistic model, the large lode pits contribute 3 million of the 3,050,000 total or more than 98%. Apportionment into a larger number of size categories would not cause much change in the estimate of total volume. (6) p - 62

After an exhaustive study of the literature where Dr. Guthrie developed estimated depths and sizes of the mines, he confirmed that Bastian's calculations for the average size of the mine (1500 cubic feet) are essentially the same as his 1590 cubic feet. Thus verifying Bastian's work, both he and I will assume 1500 cubic feet is as accurate as we can now get.

New Volume Estimates

The following estimated number of mines seems to have been a more realistic estimate than that of DuTemple's work. Using Bastian's estimate that there could have been about 1,500 with 2,000 as a top limit, and Drier's estimate of 3,000, Dr. Guthrie settled for 2,000 lode type mines on Isle Royal. In addition he estimated 3,000 more on the Houghton Peninsula and mainland. Considering this, five thousand pits seemed very possible, with maybe 2,000 more from Minnesota and Canada. Together these make up the top estimate of 7,000.

Estimates of Copper Mined / Lake Superior Region

	No. Mines	Volume Cu. ft.	% Copper in Rock	Pounds Mined
Minimum	3000	1000	0.5	3 Million
Most Likely	5000	1500	1.3	20 Million
Maximum	7000	2000	3.0	84 Million
DuTemple	5000	9425	10(a)	940 Million

(a) Actually 5 - 15 %, resulting in 500 million to 1500 million pounds of copper. All calculations assume rock is 200 pounds per cubic ft. (cubic feet.)   Ref Table 1, (6) p-61

Dr. Guthrie's "*Most likely estimate*" of 20 million pounds, I believe, creates a reasonable, conservative estimate of the amount of copper that could have been mined by the natives in the Lake Superior region. One reason I would call the estimate conservative is this: He used 1.3 percent for the ore value. He did this based on recent mining percentages. The trouble as I see it: Modern mining uses large machines, with big buckets; the rock is blasted with dynamite, etc. Consequently, these types of procedures are bound to include more of the trap rock surrounding ore bodies than the careful hammering of the ancient miners. This alone could increase the ore percent to the 3 % upper limit of his estimate.

Not including the pits in Minnesota and Ontario, and using 1.3 % ore estimates makes his assumptions conservative. I am as much at a loss as he, in being able to quantify this further. However, with two changes, say the extra 1000 pits and 3 % copper, the estimate could exceed 50 million pounds. Also, as I have stated earlier, modern mines have removed 12 billion pounds from the region and there is a lot of copper left.

I am very grateful for Dr. Jim Guthrie's generous contribution. Otherwise, I may have followed in the tracks of earlier investigators in overestimating the copper ten fold. Considering this new data I can, now, with some confidence, say the copper removed could likely range between 20 and 50 million pounds.

Timeframe Evidence

The following dates are a matter of record. They have been noted here to set the time the actual mining took place with as much accurately as possible. (4) P-38

Carbon Dating from Isle Royal in Michigan, USA

Minong Site, Copper Mine:	*2470bc +_ 150 yr.*
Minong Site, Copper Mine:	*2450bc +_ 150 yr.*
Lookout Site, Copper Mine:	*2160bc +_ 130 yr.*
Minong Site, Copper Mine:	*1850bc +_ 250 yr.*
Minong Site, Copper Mine:	*1510bc +_ 130 yr.*
Siskiwit Site, Copper Mine:	*1420bc +_ 130 yr.*
Minong Site, Copper Mine:	*1410bc +_ 130 yr.*
Minong Site, Copper Mine:	*1370bc +_ 130 yr.*
Minong Site, Copper Mine:	*1360bc +_ 130 yr.*
Minong Site, Copper Mine:	*1050bc +_ 130 yr.*
Lookout Site, Copper Mine:	*850bc +_ 120 yr.*

As is evidenced from these carbon dates, it is apparent that the copper mines of Isle Royal, Michigan were being mined, more or less, continuously for 1600 years, with the bulk of the activity in the twelve hundred years between 2400 and 1200 BC. This then becomes the window in which we will look for the cultures, which are responsible.

Repercussions from the extreme age carbon dating revealed were soon to follow. It was apparent the carbon dating technology was punching holes in the old, well-established archaeological ideas about these mines.

2 *Who Might Have Done It*

To do this amount of mining, people needed a reason. Normally, we put this kind of discussion into a supply and demand scenario. If I am hungry, I work for food or if cold, I build a shelter. Therefore, I work for something that has a direct bearing on my wellbeing. This creates the demand. If something has no direct bearing on my lifestyle, the connection must be indirect. This is the essential element of economics: I am willing to work for one thing, so I can trade it to someone else for what I want or need. Demand must always be there; otherwise, I will not put forth the effort.

I perceive this in much the same way that Mr. DuTemple did. As quoted earlier, someone had to have a very good reason to invest that much time and effort—work—for such a long duration. As an enterprise, it probably would far exceed the construction of one of the pyramids. In that regard, this should be considered one of the wonders of the world. History, as yet, does not seem to grasp the significance of this feat.

Existing Theory

Old Copper Culture, (Middle to Late Archaic Period)

Archaeologists tell us about a group of people they believe did the mining. It has always been attested that this group was acting alone in the venture. These people fit within "*the archaic tradition*" grouping. The archaic people have three defining characteristics.

> 1. Subsistence based upon the generalized hunting of a diversity of small game species and the collecting of wild plants and plant products.
> 2. The absence of pottery containers.
> 3. Burial of the dead in natural knolls or flat cemeteries, *but not in man-made burial mounds.* (8) p - 207

This culture is reputed to have lasted in Wisconsin from 8000 BC. to about 1000 BC. According to Jim Stoltman, it is within this time, which is described as the *"Middle Stage of the archaic period (ca.3000 BC. to 1200 BC)"*, that we find a few villages that fit "*The Old Copper Complex*" category. I salute him for this next quote.

"(The Old Copper complex) I will use this term in preference to culture to emphasize how little we really know about it". (8) p - 217

This candid examination of the roll of native copper, in this clearly hunting gathering society, makes Dr. Stoltman's work a good source for an accurate description of this *Copper complex.*

The copper artifact types that are considered diagnostic of Old Copper include mainly utilitarian forms (weapons and tools) used, apparently, for such tasks as hunting (spear points with a diversity of hafting devices including sockets and stems); fishing (harpoons, hooks, and gorges); wood-working (an abundance of forms presumably so used are variously referred to as spuds, Celt's, axes, adzes, chisels, gouges, and wedges); and the performance of every day household chores (single-edged knives, awls, punches drills and spatula). (8) p-218, 219

G - 5 Points and Awls, Author's Photo

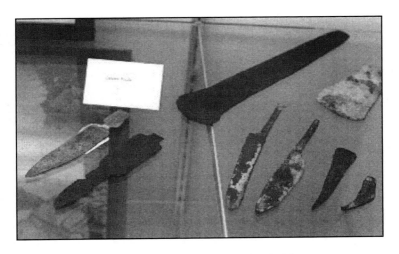

G - 6 Knives, and Points, Author's Photo

"Among the few artifacts that served an ornamental function, primarily as personal adornment, are tabular and spherical, C-shaped bracelets, a pendent, and a headdress adorned with sheet copper strips."
(8) p -219

Cracks in the old Paradigm

Two artifact types, semi-lunar or crescent-shaped knives and spear points, with a contracting stem that has multiple notches, merit special mention for they have been the source of some controversy *over a possible Eskimo origin of the Old Copper complex. The semi-lunar knife is identical to the slate or copper Eskimo women's knife (lulu), used widely throughout the American Arctic for hide working and cutting of meat and fish. Multiple-notched, stemmed spear points of polished slate occur archaeologically in the Eastern Artic in the Dorset Culture, which dates from about 800 B.C. to well after the time of Christ. Since we now know that the Old Copper complex predates the earliest known archaeological occurrences of these two artifact types in the Arctic east of Alaska by as much as 1000 years, there is no longer any basis for the Eskimo origins hypothesis. George Quimby, who has done considerable research and writing on the Old Copper complex, has just reversed this argument, suggesting that the Old Copper people retreated northward with changing floral conditions where they eventually passed their ideas on to some Eskimo groups. Quimby's hypothesis has met with little acceptance, however, because of the enormous temporal and spatial gaps that still exist in the archaeological record between the putatively related cultures. (8) p – 219,220*

But let's take a closer look at one of the more problematic issues, such as: What would the hunting and fishing native groups who are found in the Lake Superior Region do with 50,000,000 pounds of copper? Especially, since much of it is in large chunks, many weighing 20 to 100 lbs, and some as heavy as several thousands pounds. This is the root question, because if they did anything but trade, the copper would still be here. The answer is obvious—either they didn't do it, or they traded the copper away.

If these North American Indians, as we know them, didn't mine the copper on Lake Superior alone, then who did, or who helped them? That is the essential question of this book. I believe I can prove who did the mining, and why. It is no longer suitable to continue accepting the big lie we are being told about these mines.

Let's go back to James Stoltman's article in *Wisconsin Archaeology* for more on the *Old Copper complex*. After much discussion, if the *Old Copper complex* was dated to the pre-Nipissing stage of Lake Superior, or after he states, "*should thus be kept open... evidence leads to the logical conclusion that Old Copper in our region dates to the interval from about 2300 BC to 1200 BC*". (8) p - 225 One more very important piece of information from Mr. Stoltman's article needs to be brought out .

For reasons not yet understood, the period following 1200 BC witnessed a notable decline in the use of native copper to manufacture everyday tools. From this time on copper appears sporadically in Wisconsin archaeological record, but with the exception of awls and an occasional knife, most copper artifacts seems to have been designed primarily for personal adornment, for example, beads ear ornaments, rather than for utilitarian use. Accompanying this apparent decline in reliance upon native copper was a notable shift in projectile point styles from the various Middle Archaic side-notched forms to generally stemmed forms. The overall life-way, however, was still based on a seasonal round of hunting and gathering.   (8) p- 227.

What happened in 1200 BC? Why did the mining drop off drastically? Why did these locally involved natives go back to their old way of life? Keep these questions in mind, as we look further into this mystery.

New Manpower Estimates

To discover how much effort really would be needed to mine 50 million pounds of copper, we again go to Bastian's crew back in the 1960s. Based on his estimates, about 5000 man-years of work would be needed. Then, we need to double it, because the sample included only the hammering time, not cutting the firewood, fixing the meals, hunting, or fishing for the food. However, the work on Isle Royal was seasonal. Probably, at best, it was a two-month work season with one month going in, and at least one month getting the ore out. This means we need to add an amplifier of six or an estimated 60,000 person-years involved.

Now this went on for a period of about 1200 years, but since demand is never stable and a round trip took three years, we can assume there may have been about 400 active mining years. (60,000 people, divided by 400 years. = 150 people involved per year) This now seems like a very workable economic venture, but who did it?

The Problem

In my view, it is quite possible to visualize five or six Algonquin villages putting together a crew of 30 people, who trekked for a month up to Lake Superior, mined all summer, and then trekked back out with their gigantic piles of copper—**but what then? They couldn't eat it in the winter. They had used up their gathering season. Where was the demand? Where was the lifestyle improvement to justify the work? What was the motive? And, most of all, where was the copper, the tools and kettles?**

We must remember, these were hunter-gatherer people. In 2400 BC, when this started, there were not the large social groups like the Hopewell or the Mississippian Cultures. Even in Central and South America, the Olmec Culture had not yet started. **What then were these Native Indians supposed to do with thousands of pounds of copper? The trouble is right here. This is where my acceptance of the old paradigm breaks down. I can no longer picture the process. There must be a more realistic scenario to fit the facts of the story.**

Problem one: Why would they mine the copper for twelve hundred years and then stop, if their lifestyle didn't change?

Problem two: Where is the copper?

I believe the *Old Copper complex* sites are related to the early extensive mining period. However, I also believe a more realistic scenario must include a second culture. The facts point to an amalgam of two cultures that were both able to mutually benefit from the mining association. One culture (*Our Old Copper Culture*) received some very good tools and technologies, possibly fabrics and garments: while the other (Unknown culture) got the copper. If this type of trade existed for a long period, but then abruptly ceased, it would answer both problems one and two. This is what I intend to prove. The question now becomes is there evidence of a second culture? If so, what culture?

3 *Mining Evidence - Lake Superior*

Whenever anyone tries to solve a mystery, he needs to pull together the evidence at the scene. For us, this is a large area. It includes, first of all, Isle Royale National Park in Lake Superior, but after that, we need to branch out to the Houghton Peninsula and all the shores of Lake Superior. Probably, the most important place to start is the mines themselves. In the first section of the book we have described the mines, mostly from the eyes of the early discoveries. Now, we want to add important information to "hone in," if you will, on the perpetrators of this action. To me, the most logical piece of evidence with which to start is the time of the mining. Recent investigators, using the carbon dating process, have been able to determine the dates of this activity much more accurately.

The Mines

Timing: The dates mentioned in the section on mines are now a matter of record. They have been noted here to set the exact time, as well as we can, to establish that the actual mining took place. All these carbon dates were taken are on Isle Royale National Park in Michigan, USA.

As is evidenced from the carbon dates mentioned in Chapter One, it is apparent that the copper mines of Isle Royale in Lake Superior were being mined with the bulk of the activity in the twelve hundred years between 2400 and 1200 BC. This window is critical to narrow the pool of cultures that may be responsible.

We do find evidence of minor, later entries where the native peoples were using the copper for a more decorative nature. However, we will not be covering them here.

Nature of Ore Being Removed: Another piece of crucial evidence we find is the ore itself. Some of the ancient miners were moving and handling very large chunks of copper ore. A few of these were recorded before being cut up by modern day miners. Often, they weighed several thousand pounds. One such piece is on display at the Smithsonian Institute. I remember seeing another large ore chunk in front of the engineering building at the University of Minnesota in the 1960s. It was very impressive, probably five feet across, and two feet high. There were hammer marks where the ancient miners tried to knock pieces off.

We have already mentioned an interesting story, where one of these chunks had been broken free of the main ore seam and was sitting on wooden cribs a couple of feet off the bottom. It was said to have weighed nearly 12,000 pounds. It was left here. Was it too big to handle in their ships, or did the miners fail to return for it because of some unknown reason? We will never know. However, although this piece may have been too big, it must have been commonplace to remove very large pieces. Otherwise, the miners would never have even tried. The sheer size of these pieces begs the question; what could a hunting-gathering society possibly hope to do with them? They supposedly did not have the capability of smelting them down.

The next step in my investigation was to look for anything else that could be as ancient as the mines. After all, 2450 BC was about 4500 years ago. To put it into context, we need to see what the rest of the world was doing during the same approximate period. Egypt was building its first pyramid. Cities were springing up in Mesopotamia, and Stonehenge was about to be started. Aha! Here was a clue. There were some unexplained stone structures around, in relatively close proximity to the mines. Investigation led to more than I had expected.

I will start with the Megalithic stone structures. The literature tells us these structures go back about 4000 years. These large stones were used in sacred ceremonies in Ireland, England, France, Spain and other European countries throughout the Mediterranean. Many think they are about 4000 years old. I understand there are many such stones *"about 40 of them have now been located in Maine, Vermont, New York, Connecticut, and other New England states."* (9) p -1485

The Dolmens and Perched Rocks

Huron Mountain Dolmen

The next piece of local physical evidence is what is known as the Huron Mountain Mystery Stone. In point of fact, it is a dolmen. This was found and photographed by Mr. Fred Rydholm many years ago. Fred was not the first to see it. Other members of the Huron Mountain Club were already aware of its existence, when Fred first saw it as a young man.

It consists of a large boulder, *"approximately 5.7 cubic feet in volume and about 900 pounds. . . . "* that is setting on three smaller stone legs. (9) p - 1485 This particular dolmen is on the Huron Mountain Club property by Marquette, Michigan.

We took a trip to photograph this dolmen. We studied the location and took some compass shots both east and west. Two potential discoveries were made. About 180 ft. to the east, there is a pointed upright stone that may mark the sunrise at the equinox, and to the west, it appears, the equinox sun may set in a notch of the horizon a few miles away.

G - 7 Huron Mt. Dolmen, Author's Photo

This dolmen is located in the N1/2 of NE1/4 Section 25, T-52N, R-29W, and three to four hundred feet east of the crest of the mountaintop that is marked by an altitude benchmark. It is on the south side of the crest about 30 feet south of the trail.

A Swedish Dolmen

A very similar dolmen was found and photographed in Sweden by Fred Rydholm. He graciously allowed me to show it here.

G - 8 Dolmen from Sweden Courtesy, Fred Rydholm

Sawbill Landing Dolmen

On the Michigan trip, Mr. Chuck Bailey showed my friend and I photographed of a second dolmen in northern Minnesota, a little bigger than the one we visited. It is a very complex site with several features. There is also a standing stone and at least one other feature in the vicinity of the dolmen. There are two Ogham symbols on the Dolmen, a single line -"B" and a double line - "L" (see sketch). This is the common usage for the sun god, "Baal," found also at the Linderoth Site and others.

It is located in northern Minnesota's Superior National Forest, west of Sawbill Lake. The description is as follows: SE¼ of SW ¼, Section 24, T63N, R5W, in the NW corner of the 40 acre parcel: about one mile west is Kelso Lookout, Kelso Mountain. Very near this is a standing stone. The site has been surveyed and is in the records of, The Institute for the Study of American Cultures (ISAC).

This dolmen is on a small island just south of Lujcnida Lake with a perched rock on the north shore and a perched rock on the south shore, all three forming a north south line. The use of these perched rocks, in association with these dolmens, means the perched rocks by themselves are significant, if found in association with copper or a shipping activity; such as Ogham Script, copper artifacts, or harbor bore holes.

The dolmen might be in this location to identify the crossing of the divide between Lake Superior and the Hudson Bay drainage system, or it may mark a trail to a high point just to the west where Baal was honored. We can only guess. I located it and photographed it in the fall of 1997.

G - 9 Sawbill Landing Dolmen, Author's Photo

On the backside of this dolmen, there are three deep manmade groves; the first is sort of alone and the next two are together. These are generally interpreted to be B L in Ogham script. Since they do not show up well on the photo, I have just made the sketch on the left.

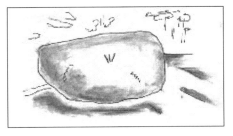

G – 10 Sketch of Baal Marks on Sawbill Landing Dolmen

Other perched rocks and standing stones in the immediate area appear to mark the course into the Temperance River System for people going south. This river takes the travelers to Lake Superior. They indicate which side of the lake or water system to follow until you are safely into the Temperance Drainage.

G - 11 Perched Rocks in Area, Author's Photo

Chuck Bailey reports there is a stone ring site in NW 1/4, NE 1/4, Section 25 in the same general area. As I understand it, the Forest Service is aware of these sights. Much credit must be given to Mr. James P. Scherz and other Midwestern members of The Institute for the Studies of American Culture (ISAC). I hope, by the time this book goes to print, Jim and Chuck have formally published this find, because there is much more to it than can be mentioned here. All I need to say is this, the Sawbill Dolmen stands out as another significant monolithic site to mark the end of this journey along the trail of stones. This site sets firmly in the heart of the copper mine country.

The Monolithic Standing Stones

The Linderoth Bolder

While I was a district ranger working for the US Forest Service, I was shown another standing stone on the Sault Ste. Marie District of the Hiawatha National Forest. Although this stone is not as dramatic as the two dolmens mentioned above, it is marked with the same type of marks as the Sawbill Dolmen. These marks in Ogham (Celtic language) spell "Baal," the Sun God of the Canaanites of the Eastern Mediterranean. It is located on the top of a high ridge, which was at one time, an island in a great glacial lake. This lake would have included Lake Superior, leads to speculation that a thorough survey could yield much more.

G - 12 Linderoth Bolder, Authors **Photo**

The adjacent lime-stone outcrop does have some markings. And, a small knoll to the east could even be an earthen mound. However, the Forest Service archeologist was not interested in this type of site and would not take it seriously.

G – 13 Sketch of Marks on Linderoth Boulder

The Soo Boulder—A Monolithic Standing Stone

History tells us of a huge upright stone that was located in downtown Sault Ste. Marie, Michigan. The Indian people were said to have worshipped this stone or honored it by throwing items into the river in front of it.

I first heard of the Soo Great Boulder several years ago. I was looking at a very old Sault Ste. Marie history book published about 1850. There was a drawing and short story about this large boulder that was located in downtown Sault Ste. Marie, Michigan. If my memory serves me, the Michigan meridian was started from that point. Unfortunately, I have not been able to relocate the book that was privately owned.

I was elated to discover confirmation in the following story in a book entitled, *"I Remember When"* which was published by the *Sault Evening News* in 1923. I will quote it here:

THE GREAT BOULDER: I remember a large boulder in our yard, in fact the largest that anyone had ever seen. It was outlined with various shapes and figures, I imagine somewhat like the Pictured Rocks. It was a great curiosity for strangers and the tourists after viewing the locks usually walked over to Ridge Street to see the large boulder, each one wishing it could be transferred to their home grounds in the city where they lived. When they were building the Iroquois Hotel, the masons decided they would like to have that stone in the foundation so they built huge fires on it for several days, breaking it in small pieces and they hauled away ten cords of stone from that one boulder. They said there was almost as much of it under the ground as above. An elm was planted in the place and has grown to be a large sized tree. MRS. MARY C. BERNIER, 224 Ridge Street, Sault Ste. Marie, Michigan (11) P-11.

Devils Island Monolith

In the summer of 1991 or 1992, Dennis Dourghty and I, with a few other friends, discovered another monolithic stone monument on an island east of Sault Ste. Marie, Michigan. It has not been authenticated yet by any of the authorities. However, we believe it was used to mark an excellent harbor and deep-water channel. The large stone, about 12 feet high, had been pushed over and had cracked in half when it fell. It was located on top of a smooth glacier island, but it was not a glacial boulder.

In fact, the people who pushed it over did not remove the stones found at its base that were used to balance it. The stone was too large to have been put there by a few pranksters. It was about 2 feet thick, 3 to 4 feet wide and, 12 feet long.

*G - 14 Devils Island
Marker Sketch*

The Calendar Site

Another piece of physical evidence is what is known as a calendar site of the Sun Cultures. It is called a calendar site because it accurately announces the beginning of the New Year, which for the record, was March 21, or more precisely, the Spring Equinox (the first day of the new year in sun worshipping cultures). It has been tested and still accurately indicates the first day of spring. Actually, it proclaims both the spring and fall equinox. This site is located north of Sault Ste. Marie, Michigan, in Ontario, Canada. It is along the Lake Superior shore in a provincial park. The symbol was chipped out of the bedrock; therefore, it would have been impossible to move it there. A site takes on added significance when it is on bedrock and functions as it was originally designed.

It was found in association with some red paint markings, many of which can be found in the vicinity of Lake Superior. There is a book that documents these very well, Dewdney Selway's *Indian Rock Paintings of the Great Lakes*. I have not chosen to use them as evidence since, to my knowledge; no one has been able to date them. I personally believe they were left by the Marine Archaic or Red Paint culture. The location of these red paintings are spread throughout the copper mining areas, both in the US and Canada.

G - 15 Eye of God Symbol, Author's Photo

G - 16 Rock Cut the Symbol is in, Author's Photo

I have visited the site several times at the equinox, both spring and fall. Each time, it functions the same. Between two and three p.m. in the afternoon, the sun in the southwest sky would reach down into the crevasse. A distinct rock-point, about one and one half feet wide on the south wall, would cast a shadow on the north wall. As the sun moved west, the shadow moved east toward the symbol. As they met, the shadow just touched the bottom of the symbol. I have shown the progression in the drawing below.

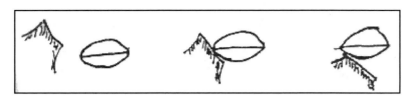

G - 17 Drawing of Eye of God, Author's Sketch

To check how precisely this recorded the actual days; I visited the site two days after the Fall Equinox one year. I was surprised to find the shadow now covered almost four inches of the symbol. Knowing this, I can easily see how the equinox day could be selected exactly.

As I stated earlier, the symbol is located on bedrock in a deep crevasse. It works as well today as it did 4000 years ago with one exception. There is more ice and snow in the crevasse.

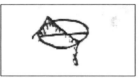

G - 18 Drawing of the Shadow on Symbol, Author's Sketch

An interesting side note, that will be shown to be important later, is that the Cree People on the Rocky Boy Reservation still have a symbol in their language, similar to the equinox symbol. The only difference is theirs has sun symbol in the top and a moon in the bottom, half day and half night (equal day and night). Their symbol is shown below. This is not a conflict. It just affirms what the symbol means in a clearer way.

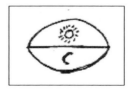

G - 19 Drawing of Cree Symbol, Author's Sketch

The Ontario Provincial Park managers were aware of the symbol. They located it about 12 years before I did. However, they did not know what it was.

Copper Artifacts General

Copper Artifact Milwaukee Public Museum, Technologies

Below are photos from West's Book, *Copper: Its Mining and Use by the Aborigines of the Lake Superior Region, Report on the McDonald Massee Isle Royal Expedition.* West recorded a number of copper culture artifacts by photograph. These photographs are of high quality. I do believe, as they did, they accurately represent the culture we are talking about here. The photos being reprinted here, courtesy of the Milwaukee Public Museum, Milwaukee County Wisconsin. (2) Plate 7867-a.

There are several significant bits of information I would like to point out about these artifacts. First, the spear points appear to have a hole designed for riveting on the handle. This is a technical advance of which I was previously unaware. The one spear-point is also of a much different design. It is four-sided which may have been done to increase the strength. The tang, made for mounting the handle, is more like those used in modern times. They would have been used with a ring or wrapping to mount the handle.

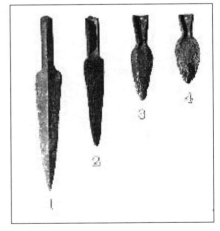

G - 20 Spear Points from Copper culture

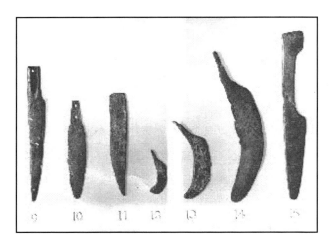

**G - 21 Knives of Copper Culture, Courtesy of
Milwaukee Public Museum**

The knives also have the riveting technologies as shown on Item 9 and 10, Graphic 21. There seems to be three other designs. Item 11 probably had a direct wrapping on the handle, while Items 12, 13 and 14 were tang-mounted. The last knife, Item 15 had a full handle-wrapping reminiscent of more modern knives. A knife with this much difference design could indicate a mixed culture.

Below is a photograph from a Museum in Alpena, Michigan. It also has points with holes, but this site also shows the nail or rivets in the same collection. It does not indicate if remnants of the wooden handle had actually been fastened. As can be seen on the photo on the right, nails were clearly used to attach the copper points to the handles. It seems unlikely a culture would stop using this type of technology abruptly.

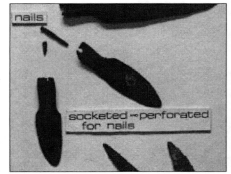

*G - 22 Nails and Points,
Author's Photo*

There was one other very interesting find at this Alpena, Michigan, Old Copper Site. The museum staff labeled it a compass for drawing circles and that is just what it looks like. It is obvious this type of artifact does not fit into what we know of archaic people. If this is a compass, what is it doing in an Ancient Copper Culture site?

G - 23 Copper Compass found on Site in Alpena, Michigan

Woodworking Tools

The axes and gouges found in these assemblages indicate the tools that would be need to cut the volumes of firewood the miners would have used. However, these are the type of tools that the Wisconsin Copper Complex people stopped using in 1200 BC, as they reverted back to their hunting and gathering lifestyle.

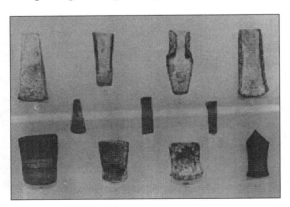

G - 24 Wood Working Tools, Courtesy of Milwaukee Public Museum

Religious Artifacts

    The Copper Snake: This small, beautifully crafted, copper snake was found in the local museum in Sault Ste. Marie, Ontario, Canada. It is only about 6 to 7 inches long and very delicately done. It was located at the Glacial Lake Nipissing Beach a few miles west of Sault Ste. Marie, Ont. It is one more piece of ancient religious evidence. The Nipissing Beach was created about 1500 BC.

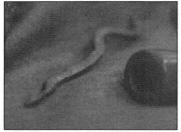

G - 25 Copper Snake, Author's Photo

    This type of piece would have been common to worshippers of Isis or Ishtar, the female Canaanite and Minoan goddess, who controlled nature. To my knowledge, native people of more modern times did not craft snake symbols or idols. Nevertheless, some of the mound culture people must have used snakes (Serpent Mound) in their religious culture. As stated earlier, these mound cultures did not exist in 1500 BC, the association date of the small copper snake artifact. Yet they may well be cultural descendants of some of the miners.

G - 26 Graphite Snakes, One Copper sheeted, Author's Photo

    In New London, Connecticut, we find a rather unusual artifact. It has been identified as being from a 4000-year-old Red Paint Site. The artifacts are located in the Washington County Museum. The most important find was a double-twisted snake carved in graphite. One of the snakes was believed to have been covered with small sheets of copper that were fastened with small pegs. The importance of this site is both the date and the copper. It does help use to make the connection to the New England Red Paint People. The other finds, three carved plummets, will be explained later.

Double Ax

The Double Ax found in this collection is extremely important to attest to the real identity of the miners. Like the snake, it is a religious symbol that can be traced back to the early Minoan culture. Here, we have it showing up in the hands of our hunting-gathering people in Wisconsin and Michigan.

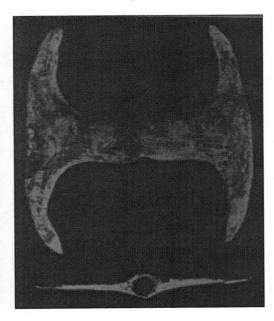

G - 27 Wisconsin Double Bit Ax Photo, Courtesy of, the Milwaukee Public Museum of Milwaukee County

Morrison Island Find

A large find of 250 copper artifacts on Morrison Island, in the middle of the Ottawa River Valley, is worth mentioning. It was found in burials and along with an occupation site. One part of the site dates to 2700 BC, which makes it our earliest actual carbon dated site. There also was a beveled spear point without a socket, like the one that was mentioned earlier. There also was a supply of un-worked copper that could indicate a manufacturing site or a trade center.

We will get a better description if we quote Griffin directly concerning Morrison Island:

> *For the first time at a site with such a large amount of copper there was also a considerable amount of bone, stone and flint material and these have a strong relationship to sites of the Late Archaic Laurentian cultures of the upper St. Lawrence-New York area. There are harpoons with barbs on one side only, with the large specimens having a line hole near the base. There are eyed bone needles, awls, gorges, an ulu-shaped knife and a little flute fragment. Over 200 beaver teeth had been employed as chisels. There were a large number of grindstones and small pieces of fine-grained sandstone had a ground cutting or sawing edge. There were stone gouges, celts, a plummet and projectile points similar to Lamoka and Brewerton side-notched" (Ritchie 1961). (Dyck and Fyles, 11961 P 180) (GSC – 162) . . . "Most of the recovered Old Copper artifacts in Ontario were concentrated along the lake Nipissing-Ottawa river waterway, and along the Trent river waterway from Georgian Bay to the mouth of the St. Lawrence." Ref Griffin p – 283,284*

Newberry Find—Statues and Tablet

The Newberry Tablet

The Newberry Tablet is one piece of physical evidence that is only partially available. However, we have substantial sworn testimony and photographs that it did, in fact, exist in 1896. It was judged to be fraudulent at the time, apparently because it was not understood, and was beyond the comprehension of the experts. This document was found with three statues, parts of which can still be found in the Fort De Beuade Museum in St. Ignace, Michigan.

My first experience, with what I will call "The Newberry Tablet" or "McGruer's Gods", came when I asked a friend of mine, a local historian, if he had ever heard of any ancient texts. He said he had heard of a tablet, supposedly found in the Newberry area many years ago, but he had not followed up on the story.

Mary Linderoth is very knowledgeable on the subject and gave me numerous books and articles referring to it. One of the old newspaper articles she had, pertaining to the Newberry Tablet, did an excellent job of whetting my interest. I will quote a little of it here: (the following quotes were taken from an old newspaper article, barely legible and from an unidentified newspaper). The headline read:

BY WHO'S HANDS WERE THE IMAGES AND TABLET PLACED IN THE WOODS NEAR NEWBERRY, THE IMAGES FACE EAST, THIS FACT POINTS STRONGLY TO SUN WORSHIP, Newberry, Mich. Nov.28-Special-The discovery made a few days ago near here promises to rank in importance second to nothing yet unearthed, relating to the prehistoric age in this country.

This early reporter was very correct in his analysis of the importance of these finds. However, universities and scientific intellectuals of the time could not deal with the magnitude of what really was found. It was judged a fake and dismissed as a backwoods hoax. But, let's get back to this article:

Jacob Brown and George Rowe, both residents of Newberry, were looking for deer, and in the course of their hunt startled a mink, which made for a swamp near by and took refuge in a hollow stump. In digging under one side of the stump in order to get the mink, they struck stone which bore evidence of the handy work of man. Becoming interested, they secured a pick and spade and unearthed the stones.

As a result of their labors, three stone images were uncovered, also a large stone tablet. All four articles were cut from brown sandstone, the rock probably coming from the north-westward, where the pictured rocks, great cliffs of sandstone, worn by wind and wave, into fantastic forms known for many miles upon the blue water of the great lake.

The editor of this big city paper (possible Detroit or Toledo) decided to embellish the story. Soon, he gets back to it and goes on like this:

Of the three images, the largest is that of a man in a sitting posture, nearly life size. The statue is on a pedestal formed from the same piece of stone. The second image from (?) point of size is that of a woman and is a trifle under three feet in height. While the third is the image of a child, and like the man is postured in a sitting attitude, and is about two feet high. All three of the images were found placed with faces toward the east, which may have

been accidental, but more probably intentional, and point strongly
towards sun worship on the part of the unknown race, that carved
and placed the statues in times so distant that even an
approximate estimate of the period is impossible. (Author
underlined for emphasis)

Near the figures was found a slab of brownstone averaging six
inches in thickness and 18 x 25 inches on each face. One side was
smoothed as carefully as the course structure of the rock would
had allowed, while upon the other face were engraved a series of
inscriptions, each set in a square of approximately one and a half,
there being 140 of these.

According to the author of this article, the source was the Newberry
Times. I decided to check the local newspaper to find the original article.
As stated earlier, the one I was using came from an unknown source,
possibly Toledo, Ohio. It was not long before I found the article and was
getting a firsthand news report from the original writer. It was reported
just the way he and all the other local residents knew it happened, factual
and in his own words. Anyone who would call the story a fake really
underestimated these small town people—but here, read the reprinted
copy of the article and make your own judgment.

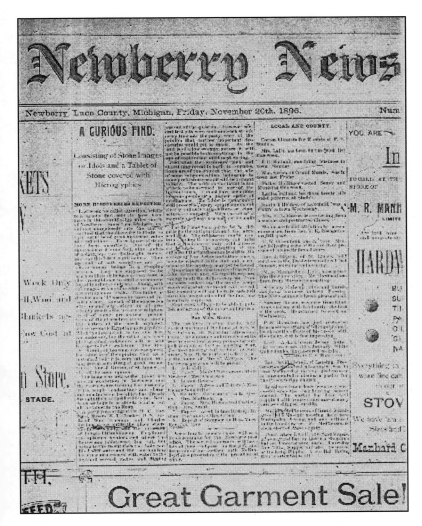

G - 28 The Original 1896 Newberry Article

THE NEWBERRY NEWS

Page Sixteen

Wednesday, November 20, 1996

TRAVELLING THROUGH TIME

by Therese Schummer

100 Years Ago - 1896

—Winter has come to stay!

—One of the boys got a shot at the Big Deer that has frequented the marsh for some time. He didn't come within a mile of hitting it though.

—Two men employed cutting wood, hunting and trapping, a few miles north of Newberry, are reported having made a curious find. While digging for a mink under the upturned root of a cedar tree, they came upon what they suppose to be the petrified remains of three persons.

They are said to be good specimens, but as no one has seen them outside of the reported finders, particulars will have to be deferred until another issue. Since writing the above, we are informed that the fossils have been brought to town and will be placed on exhibition as soon as they are set up. (11-13-1896 issue)

—Last week we called attention, briefly, to a curious find said to have been made in this county a few miles north of Newberry. Since then we have examined more closely into the matter and find that the discovery is likely to turn out to be of great historical value and importance.

Three figures of stone have been unearthed. One of the figures measures one foot, nine inches in height; one two feet, eight inches; and one three feet, eight inches. They are made of soft sandstone and resemble human beings in a stooping posture. They are supposed to be heathen idols or images as they bear a close resemblance to similar specimens found in other countries.

Along with the images was a stone slab or tablet measuring about 19 x 26. This tablet is divided into 140 spaces by lines cut into the stone. In each of the spaces is a letter or character, which in all probability records the history or religious creed of some prehistoric people. Some of the characters are very much like letters of the Greek alphabet, others resemble Egyptian hieroglyphics.

What the inscription is no one here can make out, but the tablet has been photographed and copies will be sent to experts for translation. The Rev. Dr. Howell of Lansing, who was shown the tablet, is of the opinion that as a historical relic it is very valuable and may reveal something of great importance. Rev. J. Gibson of St. Ignace is also of the same opinion.

The images, as well as the tablet, are now on exhibition in Newberry and their owners are turning the curiosity of the people to advantage and charging an admission fee which has already brought them a considerable sum. Next week we hope to be able to print a cut of the tablet in the *News*.

A party consisting of Dr. H. Farrand, Messrs. W.T. Croker, D.N. McLeod, Wm. Truman and Charles Brehner drove out to the place where the find was made with the intention of doing a little exploring. They found the upturned hemlock root where the figures and tablet were dug out, but owing to the recent thaw, the hole was filled with water and the surrounding territory also covered with water to the depth of several inches and digging was out of the question.

However, several test pits were sunk and rock struck every time and the party were of the opinion that further important discoveries would yet be made. As the land is of a low, swampy nature it will not be possible to do anything in the way of exploration until next spring.

Just what the explorers' pick and shovel may reveal is hard to surmise. Some are of the opinion that the site of some religious edifice belonging to some prehistoric people will be brought to light. ... The tablet is remarkably well-preserved; every square stands out clearly and only three letters or characters are missing. With the aid of a magnifying glass these may yet be made out.

The find may turn out to be a rich prize to the antiquarian and the archaeologist. The tablet, no doubt, contains the key to the mystery and until that is deciphered only wild guesses can be made. The attention of the officers of the Smithsonian Institute, the college at Ann Arbor and other places have been called to the find and a solution of the mystery may yet be found.

Meantime, the discoverers of the relics, Jake Gordon and George Howe, are raking in all the dollars they can from curiosity seekers, and the public keeps wondering what the tablet will reveal. But curiosity will not be fully satisfied until the neighborhood of the find has been fully explored.

Next week we hope to be able to publish a diagram of the tablet and figures.

G - 29 Newberry Article, 1996 Reprint

A follow up article in The Mining Journal Hospital Edition from Marquette indicates the excitement this find had created in rural northern

Michigan. This article included photos of the tablet and two of the three statues. It also shows a large 6000 pound piece of copper that has been worked by the ancients with hammers.

This find, is in fact, the most definite piece of evidence anywhere on this subject. Archeologists are obliged to continue to call this a fraud or else deal with its implications. To date, they have chosen to let the fraud defense stand. I will point out later, how both the statues and the text themselves make the likelihood of this very improbable, if not impossible. In fact, to my knowledge, there has never been one piece of evidence presented which points to a hoax or fraud.

At first, it seemed all of the local men of learning in the community and surrounding communities also questioned the find. However, they chose to investigate before they made a final decision. I would like to pull a quote from the previous article on this question:

> *"A party consisting of Dr. H. Farrand, Messrs. W.T. Croker, D.N. McLeod, Wm. Truman and <u>Charles Brebner</u> drove out to the place where the find was made with the intention of doing a little exploring. They found the upturned hemlock root where the figures and tablet were dug out, but owing to a recent thaw the hole was filled with water . . ." (12)*

We find the name, Charles Brebner, also as the person who supplied the photos to the Smithsonian Institute, where still today, they languish in a folder labeled Michigan Fakes. However, none that examined the artifacts or site, and who questioned the involved parties, believed the finders could have perpetrated such a hoax. In the end, they all accepted it as a tremendous find. It must have been a hard pill to swallow, when the intellectual world-at-large turned its back on these findings. It is humanity's loss that these artifacts were not valued and protected, but instead put in a leaky old horse barn where they were nearly destroyed. This one find, the Newberry Tablet, could have done much to correct our erroneous history, if it had been valued, tested and interpreted in its original condition.

Chuck Bailey, one of our ISAC Members mentioned earlier, went to the Smithsonian Institute (SI) and found the actual Newberry Tablet pho-tos—the original ones sent to the SI in 1896. I took black and white pic-tures of the photos. A lot more could be said about these statues and the tablet, but that will have to wait until later in the book. Here, we are summarizing what ancient evidence we have that seems to go back 4000 years, and does it point to a second trade culture.

G – 30 Three Statues and Newberry Tablet,
Smithsonian Institute, 1896 Charles Brebner's Photo

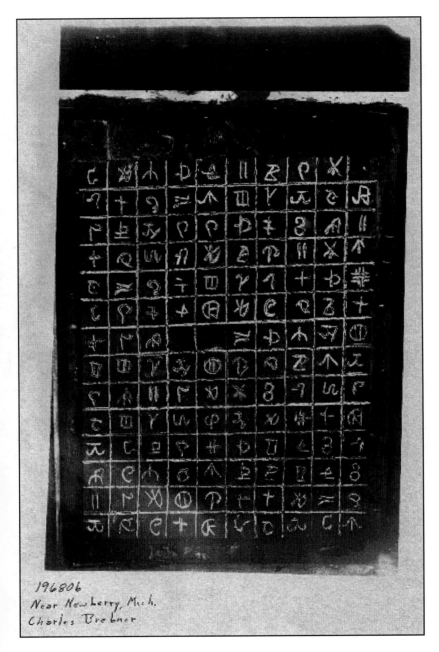

G - 31 Newberry Tablet, Charles Brebner's 1896 Photo

The Sutton Land Deed

Another bit of written historical information of significance can be found on an official deed from New Hampshire, dated 1681. Although this is east of Lake Superior, the connection will be completed in the language section, Chapter 9. The Plymouth settlement was only 51 years old that year. The natives were persuaded to sell or trade a portion of their lands to the Colonists. Many of the tribal leaders signed or affixed their marks to the deed. Of these signers, one signed his name in English—not too bad for a people portrayed as ignorant savages in later years. Several others, also, wrote the first part of their names in English. This was not the best part; nine others signed their names in their own native written language, which upon study, has been discovered to be a form of an ancient Cypriot language.

I have quoted Barry Fell to get the best interpretation:

About a dozen different alphabets were in use among the North American Indians at the time when the colonies were established three hundred years ago. Unfortunately the founding fathers paid no attention to these matters, and regarded the true native scripts that were used on the early Deeds as no more than illiterate "marks." Later on, in the early eighteen-hundreds, missionaries such as James Evans became aware of some of the Algonquian scripts, and then adopted them for teaching Christian religion. Because of this, Evans has been wrongly credited with "inventing" Cree script; what he really did was something much more praiseworthy, he made it the official method of printing the Cree language, including the entire Cree Bible—and thereby he preserved an ancient alphabet. In 1978 some stone tablets in the museums in San Sebastian and San Telmo, in the Basque provinces of Spain, were referred to me to study by Spanish scholars. I noticed that some of them including stones known to have been engraved before the time of Columbus, carried lines of letters that appeared to be identical with the Cree letters. When I substituted the sound values of the Cree letters for those signs on the Basque tablets, the resultant language that emerged proved to be Basque. I then sent translations back to Spain, and these were in turn studied by the leading Basque linguist, Imanol Agire, who is the author of major works on ancient Iberian inscriptions and on the Basque language. After Dr. Agire had studied the matter, he wrote back to me this year (1980) congratulating me on the decipherment, and confirming that it was correct. Thus now we are able to read and translate ancient Spanish inscriptions, by using the Algonquian alphabets. In the new edition of the Grand Basque Encyclopedia these important links with ancient America are stressed.

Indian owners of the land sign the Sutton Deed, and they used two different alphabets. Those who had attended the schools for Indians such as the pre-college level school in Cambridge, set up by Harvard, signed their names in English letters, either the whole name or the first few letters of the name (see figure 1). Those who preferred to use the ancient Algonquian writing system signed their names in a form of script some times called mamalohikan, in which the individual letters stand for separate syllables, and the letters themselves are those of the ancient alphabet of Cyprus. The Cypriot inscriptions, in the island of Cyprus, remained in-decipherable until 1871, when an English linguist named George Smith discovered inscriptions in Greek and Cypriot on the same stone, and was able to use this bilingual key to discover the sound values of the mysterious signs. In table 2, I have set out a series of the Nipmauq signatures, side by side with the corresponding letters of the Cypriot alphabet which, like the Cree, is also syllabic. If Smith had only known, he could have summoned Algonquians to aid him!

The Cypriot alphabet, or syllabary as it is more correctly called, was in use at least until 1727, in northern Maine, New Brunswick and Nova Scotia, for a treaty signed at Annapolis Royal, NS, in that year carries 32 Cypriot signatures. It has since died out in North America, though the Cree Syllabary on the other hand has flourished, and is used today by newspapers and magazines published in the Cree tribal lands. In recent years it has been adapted for use by the Eskimo, and some Ojibwa still use it also.

In Europe, on the other hand, the Cypriot Syllabary was no longer used after the third century BC, for Greek letters replaced it during the administration of Alexander the Great. Thus in order for it to have been brought into use in America, the alphabet must have been transmitted here before the time of Alexander. These new discoveries have, needless to say, called forth the condemnation of some archaeologists. They are however, now firmly established and have already been incorporated into the learned publications by European linguists. (10) p – 22 - 25

I have included Dr. Fell's Figure 1 and Figure 2 below:

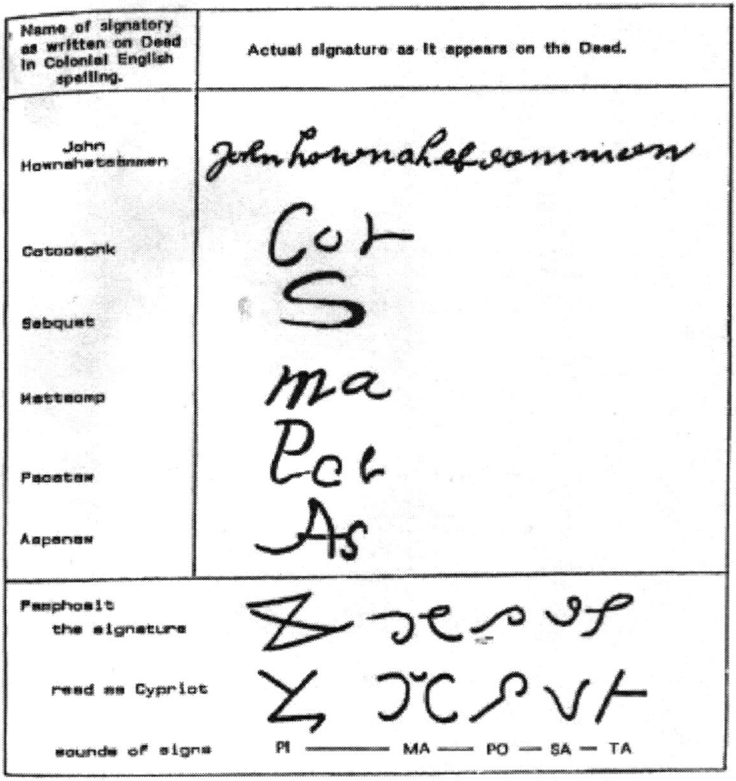

Name of signatory as written on Deed in Colonial English spelling.	Actual signature as it appears on the Deed.
John Hownshetammen	
Cotoosonk	
Sabquat	
Hattaomp	
Pacataw	
Aspanaw	
Pamphosit the signature	
read as Cypriot	
sounds of signs	PI —— MA — PO — SA — TA

FIGURE 1: The Indian signatures on the Nipmauq Deed of A.D. 1681/2 can be classified into four groups. GROUP 1, illustrated by the uppermost example, are signatures written out in full, in Colonial English – evidently the signatures of alumni of the schools established by the Colonists. GROUP 2 comprises signatures that render only the first syllable or initial letter, in English script of the signatory. GROUP 3, lowermost, signatures written out in full, not in theColonial English script, but in the ancient syllabary of Cyprus. Actually the name rendered as "Pamphosit" is erroneous, as the sound of F (PH) does that occur in the Algonquian tongues. The Cypriot rendering, on the other hand, omits the H, thus giving P in place of F. Signatures of GROUP 4 are shown in the separate tabulation of Figure 2.

G - 32 Nipmauq Signatures, Figure 1

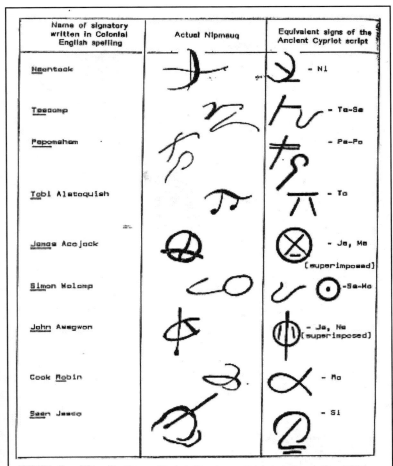

FIGURE 2:   Nine signatures, showing the correspondence between the initial syllables of the names (left column, underlined letters) with the equivalent syllabic signs of the ancient Cypriot script that died out in Europe during the time of Alexander the Great but survived in the Americas, where the script had apparently been introduced by ancient traders from the Mediterranean.

G – 33 Figure 2 Nipmauq Signatures, Figure 2

Some intellectuals chose to discount Dr. Fell's work. However, I find his material to be some of the most interesting and accurate information on this subject. Considering what he has done himself, and what he published in his Epigraphic Society Papers, a large enough amount of solid information has been presented, that is, for anyone with a mind open enough to consider it. Some confusion has arisen in the early work on this subject, due to the fact that the Adena Culture period (800 BC to 150 BC) has been mixed with much earlier (2400 BC to 1200 BC) pre-mound Old Copper Culture mining era information. This can be understood, if we realize that the early pre-Algonquian of the first period living in the northeastern United States relates to the early Cypriot/Minoan traders. The post-mining Adena Mound Culture of the Upper Mississippi Valley was heavily influenced by the Phoenician/ Libyan groups working out of Carthage in North Africa.

The Sutton Land Deed is the best evidence we have to indicate that the people using Cypriot scripts and language heavily influenced the early Algonquian people in southern New England. Perhaps, they were actually a colony of such people. We do not know which is more correct. For the purpose of this work, the point is moot. These questions will be covered more fully near the end of this book when we discuss the language proof more fully.

To summarize here, we have already found much evidence that indicates a possible connection to specific old world cultures. The dolmen and calendar sites point to a sun worshipping culture. The name Baal, carved on two local stones, seems to support a Canaanite connection. The Newberry Tablet and the Sutton Land Deed both indicate a possible Cypriot/Minoan syllabic script language connection. The copper artifacts, the snake, and the double ax both point to a possible Minoan connection about 1500 BC. Using these bits of evidence, we must turn to these old world cultures to see who had the motive and ability to mine, ship, and utilize or trade 20 to 50 million pounds of copper.

4 *The Old World Setting*

Although this is a story about the cultural heritage, resources, and people of the Lake Superior area, we must look in other parts of the world to create the proper setting. To achieve this, I will describe a little of what is going on in the Mediterranean world of this period, (4000 BC to 1200 BC). An ancient historical context is essential to understanding this work. We need to know what cultures were out there in 3000 BC, and, are they relevant to our discussion of the mining, which started in 2450 BC.

During the late Neolithic (agricultural) Period, a change slowly began to develop in the Middle East. The small Neolithic villages grew larger and more sophisticated. This was taking place in the two land areas of Egypt and Mesopotamia. The date was about 4000 BC. Egypt was still a group of smaller cites with a common culture, and Mesopotamia (the land between the rivers) was occupied by the culture known as "The Old Sumerian Culture" or Sumer. As these two cultures began what was the first truly urban society, a second and important step in evolution had begun to develop. This was a wholesale trade of raw materials. At the same time, a form of international trade between these two cultures began.

Urban society is based on whole group activities. I will just review a few of the more important ones. The most common were: potters, farmers, priests, governors, soldiers, carpenters, shipbuilders, merchants and scribes. As these labor specialties imply, the activities of making, and presumably, selling pots, houses, swords, and ships were all taking place by the year 3100 BC.

Three Existing Cultures

It was about 3100 BC when Menes, King of Upper Egypt, conquered Lower Egypt and made it into one nation. This began the reign of the rulers called pharaohs. In the same century (3100 BC), the Sumerian people, at the great city of Uruk on the Southern Mesopotamian Plain, began to use written language. It was probably caused by the need to record trade contracts for the new urban areas.

With the advent of writing we have the beginning of what we call the historic period. The time before written language is called prehistory.

Now we begin to see a third society being described. This society is made up of the city-states of the Aegean, the south shore of the Anatolian Peninsula, and the Eastern Mediterranean shore. Its culture, as far as I can tell, began to develop out of the earlier sea-going Neolithic traders. Before 3100 BC, I do not have a sense of who these people really were. They were probably made up of adventuresome Sumerian and Canaanite merchants moving out from Sumer to the west. They may have allied themselves with the hardy Neolithic fishermen along the southern Anatolian coast, the latter providing the boats and seamen expertise for the first few ventures. Some of these people will eventually be referred to as the Hittites by about 2250 BC. But for now, we should think of them as small merchant city-states, either sent out from Sumer to colonize for the purpose of trade, or people who developed from existing Neolithic villages.

It is apparent—this activity had been developing before 3100 BC, because by 3000 BC there is a culture established from Crete in the Aegean area to Cyprus in the Eastern Mediterranean and in the city-states of Ugarit, Biblos, and Sidon—the areas known as the Levant. At the time, the people went by the name of their city-state, such as "the Sidonians". But for now I will use Arthur Evans' name for the culture. He called them "the Minoan People", named after King Minos of the now famous city of Knossos on Crete. He was the first archaeologist to really publish a description of these people. The Minoan group was only one of the rich merchant trader kingdoms. Other historians say the name Minoans originated from the "Minitar" (half-man and half-bull) that they worshipped.

One of the major markets for these trade ships was the Canaanite city of Ugarit. Here the copper ore was smelted into the distinctive copper ingots shaped somewhat like a sheep's hide. This ingot was a basis for exchange at the time, almost like money.

Both Crete and Cyprus were involved in this shipping business. We find the connection of these two island cultures, not only in their trade, but also in their written Cypriot/Minoan script. Here, again, Evans showed the relationship between the Minoan script linear b and the Cypriot script.

These very early pre-alphabetic written language scripts are called, Syllabaries. This means the script does not use an alphabet, as we know it, with consonants and vowels. Instead it has about 40 to 50 sounds or syllables, each of which has a sign or symbol. It is important to understand the key differences here between this and alphabetical writing. Later in this book, I will show how the written syllabic language was then modified and simplified to provide the basic trade language.

This would enable the scribes to write down the basic sounds of any spoken language, at least adequately to carry on the organized trade.

The commercial hub between the Mesopotamian area, Egypt, and the developing Hittite culture on the Anatolian peninsula, was Ugarit. At this great trade center, they used no less than ten languages, and at least five different scripts at the cultural peak. It was probably here, since Canaanite interpreters and scribes would have been in great demand, that the Sumerian Cuneiform Syllabary was blended with the idea of hieroglyph like symbols, making the two similar scripts (Linear A & B) used on Crete and Cyprus.

As we move through the first half of the third millennium BC (3000 BC to 2500 BC), we see the maturation of these three cultures. As yet, around other parts of the Middle East, Europe, and Asia, the Neolithic cultures still are prevalent. This is of primary importance since at the end of this period (2450 BC); the first copper mines were opened up on the island of Isle Royale in Lake Superior.

Description of the Three Cultures

Now look a little more closely at the three cultures we find at this period of time. Although they go by many different names in many different languages, we will refer to them as follows: Egyptian, the Nile River Valley, Sumerian, Mesopotamia, the Tigris and Euphrates River Valleys, Cypriot/Minoan, the islands of the Aegean Sea, and Cyprus, Semitic, Ugarit, and all city-states of great wealth in the Levant (the Eastern Mediterranean Shore). These two urban cultures and one confederation of trading city-states from the Aegean Sea to the Eastern Mediterranean Sea, make up the literate world during the 500-year period from 3000 BC to 2500 BC.

It should be noted here that there were Neolithic villages and towns over a much broader area. They had already reached as far as Ireland. These villages were developing skilled tradesmen—obviously boat and shipbuilders, metal workers, potters, farmers and others. The major difference was the absence of urbanization, written language, and high volume trade in natural resources used in manufactured commercial goods (international commerce).

Description of Egypt of 2500 BC

The Egyptian culture began to show a national status when King Menes united Upper and Lower Egypt in 3100 BC. This was at the time of the first and second Dynastic periods. It also featured the start of the first building of a pyramid at Cheops. This great pyramid of Giza, Egypt, was reported to have been built in 2570 BC during the fourth Dynasty of the Egyptian Pharaohs. It is the largest pyramid in the world and was built for the Egyptian King Khufu. It was built only a scarce 120 years before the first mines were made on Lake Superior (Kitchi-Gummi).

We are all quite aware of the Egyptian culture, so I will not spend a lot of time describing it. I will say, like the Mesopotamia, it is on a rich river valley, the Nile. The surplus grain had allowed for the development of cities as well as large religious and governmental organizations. Men and resources were available for administrative projects, which made it possible to build the large temple to the Sun God at Karnack.

The Egyptians wrote in hieroglyphs, which started about 3100 BC. Some believe the concept of written language was imported from Sumer where it had begun. However, only the concept could have been used, because the language bears no other resemblance. There are symbols for about 24 consonant sounds. The vowels are not used, but implied. They recorded the words on papyrus, a sort of reed paper.

Copper and bronze were used for a large numbers of tools—from small items like holders of the scribes' pens, to large chains, gate hinges, and armor. Of course, weapons of war, swords, and chariots were also first made of copper and then bronze. Their technology was on a par with Sumer, if not better in some things.

The Egyptian religion was quite complex with many gods. Horus, and Amon Ra (Ra) are two you may have heard of. The temple at Karnack is of a solar and astronomical design. The Hyksos period in Egypt, which lasted approximately 200 years between 1750 and 1550 BC, was a time when both the Egyptian and Canaanite cultures worshipped Ra. The worship of Ra (a sun god) was similar to the religion of Sumer in the 19 century BC. Some of the Canaanites lived in the eastern Nile Delta, better known as the land of Goshen in the Bible (Joseph's time). The Canaanites worshipped the sun god Anu and his consort Isis. Here, Isis was also represented by the snake in some forms and, the bull was considered sacred. However, we do not find evidence of bullfights or rituals, such as jumping over the bull. This is probably because, after the Hyksos period the old multi-god religion was re-instituted.

Because Egyptians did such an exceptionally good job of documenting their history, we now have solid evidence of some of the first large ships and boats. As early as the time of Cheops (3960 to 3908 BC), large ships were being constructed. One large ship weighed a total of 700 tons when loaded with the two huge stone Obelisks. This model below was found in one of the early tombs.

**G - 34 Boat
Model from
Tomb, Authors
Photo, British
Museum**

Description of Sumer of 2500 BC

I need to describe the people living in southern Mesopotamian, the culture known as the Sumerians. This was at a time when urbanization was first being developed, about 3000 BC, until about 1800 BC, when they stopped speaking the Sumerian language.

These dates are generally considered to start in the Uruk period, 3400 BC or earlier. For the first time, we see a four-tiered society—cities, towns, villages, and hamlets. This society exhibited the first urbanization, a specialized society—armies, farmers, masons, and others. This was probably caused by one of the old standbys, surplus grain crops—due to more sophisticated irrigation which resulted in more spare-time and increased population. Improvements in the genetics of seed grain made food production easier. The social organization of the time was independent city-states and their surrounding villages. Each city had its own member in the pantheon of gods:

> We have already indicated that in the Uruk period the temple seems to have been the dominant institution, but the period may have seen the emergence of the first secular rulers. The evidence is scanty but we have the depiction in the art of a bearded figure that is not a priest, wearing a type of Pathan hat. We also probably have the word Sharru, the Arcadian word for king, in a syllabary of the late Uruk period. (17) P-21

> Not all of the cities were ruled by Sumerian princes: Kish in the north of the plain was apparently the home of a Semitic dynasty from the earliest of times. (17) P-21

A list of important cities was as follows: Adab, Lagash, Larsa, Ur, Uruk, and Eridu. Each of these cities had their own special god who was supposed to defend them. Ishtar had her home at Uruk that also, housed the sky god Anu. The Ziggurat at Ur was just one of the staged towers that dominated the major cities. The bible references the tower of Babel where, God created the many languages to create confusion. This is surely how the urban centers of Sumer must have seemed to the Nomadic Semitic herdsmen from the surrounding hills.

G - 35 The Ziggurat, Author's Sketch, (17) p - 75

Another part of Sumer's religious culture was the ever-present golden calf or the sacred bulls of this culture.

G - 36 Naram Sin, Wearing Horns of Divinity (17) p - 17

A second religious symbol of the Sumerians is the snake of Ishtar. These symbols of the female, earth mother's, rejuvenative powers represented the fertile regenerative nature of Mother Earth. After all, the snake does create a new skin as it grows.

These symbols are found in all three centers, Sumer, Egypt, and Crete. However, we have no pictures of Egyptians wearing the horns of divinity. In fact, when the Egyptians portray the sea people, they show them wearing the horn helmets.

G - 37 Map of Sumer, Author's Sketch (17) p-22

The old Sumerian culture finally succumbed to total Semitic domination. Scholars use the reign of Hammurabi, King of Babylon, as the convenient breaking point where Semitic take-over of the Mesopotamian Valley was complete. This is known as the Ascension of Hammurabi. Actually, the Semitic people and the people of Sumer lived adjacent to each other for many centuries in apparent peace.

Some of the major items the Sumerian culture probably invented were the wheel, the true arch, the corbel vault, and the dome. Their counting system is still in use today. It divides the hour into sixty minutes and sixty seconds, respectively, and the circle into 360 degrees.

The urban revolution led to the first industrial revolution, or maybe the reverse was true. Since trade is of essence in our story, we need to look at the major items of industry and trade in Sumer. Although we cannot state which industries were the biggest, it is clear the following were very big. Grain was probably the largest export. The second most important was probably textiles. The temples or palaces apparently owned the factories. Sheepskin is also in evidence on some of the statues. Other sheep related items were used.

The high, so-called polos headdresses worn by the priestesses of Mari may have been made of felt, illustrating another manufacturing skill which would be reasonable to find in an economy where sheep were so important and where long standing ties with Nomadic herdsman. (17) P-126

The technology of the horizontal loom is evident on a seal of 300 BC. This could represent carpet making.

Pottery was in abundance. Sometimes, it was mass-produced. However, it is not clear if it was also made in smaller, family size batches. The higher quality items were traded to surrounding villages but the trade was probably local.

Large-scale metalworking seems to have been done mostly by the public sector. These smiths had a high level of technical skills. There is evidence of casting, using the lost wax process:

> *The archeological remains indicate a rapid increase in the use of metals from protoliterate times, with copper and lead being the most widely used metals. (17) P-131*
>
> *It is usually assumed that metals were imported into Sumer already smelted, probably in the form of ingots, to avoid the expense and difficulty of transporting quantities of useless rock to a country almost devoid of the fuel necessary for smelting. (17) P-131*
>
> *The suddenness of the increase in the use of metals at the end of the fourth millennium and the rapid increase in technological skills suggest the possibility that contact with craftsmen from areas outside Mesopotamia, with a longer metallurgical tradition, may have been a factor in the development. . . . True tin bronze is only widely used in the second half of the third millennium (2500 BC to 2000 BC).* (17) p - 132

This may be explained by the tin resource being discovered in the British Isles at about this time. It could also be assumed that the development of the Cypriot/Minoan trading culture in 3000 BC, including the Canaanite city of Ugarit on the mainland just across from Cyprus, may have provided the technology and the resources necessary. A very large amount of smelting was done there if one estimate (200,000 tons) is right. We know that Ugarit was also a major smelting city since kilns and molds for the distinctive copper ingots were found there. Ugarit and Cyprus were probably the main sources for Egyptian copper. At the same time, it would have been only a short ride to the headwaters of the Euphrates and a float down to Sumer.

Like Egypt, the Sumerian urban culture needed raw materials to produce their trade goods. They also needed markets for their wool fabrics, warm felts, and sheepskin over garments.

Copper and tin were also needed to make bronze for the tools and weapons. As each city-state struggled to hold onto their lands, a variable arms race took place. Swords, daggers, shields, and helmets were mass-produced under the direction of Hammurabi, one of the Semitic kings around 1800 BC. Over time these struggles degenerated into all-out wars. This would have been an ideal situation for the island traders, kept secure by their dominance of the sea, to prosper from the international copper and tin trade.

They had the economic structure necessary to procure these raw materials. This can be confirmed by some quotes taken from tablets on the *Law in Mesopotamia* from Sumer. They are from a period about 2000 BC to the creation of Hammurabi Empire. There were price controls, wage controls, and fixed penalties for theft, day or night. Listen to these laws, and you will see a very ordered society:

1. *1 Kor of Barley is (priced) at 1 shekel.*
2. *3 QA of the "best oil" are (priced) at one shekel of silver.*
3. *3 minnas of copper are (priced) at 1 shekel of silver.*
4. *2 minnas of refined copper are priced 1 shekel of silver.*
5. *The hire of a boat is 2 QA per kor (of capacity) 1 seah, 1 qa is the hire for the boatmen. He shall drive it the whole day.*
6. *The wages of a hired man are one shekel of silver; his provender is 1 pan of barley. He shall work for one month (30 days).*
7. *A man caught in the field of a Muskenum (social class connected with the palace) in the crop during daytime, shall pay 10 shekels of silver. He who is caught in the crop at night, shall die, he shall not get away alive. (20) p - 133*

The laws go on to state things such as: a slave cannot make an investment with the official state finance officer. This implies that a free holder can. If a man takes the slave girl of another, and she dies in his house, he must replace her with two more slave girls. If a man breaks another man's hand in a fight, he shall pay ½ minna of silver. Sixty of the laws are listed on the tablets that have been located. These laws are very comprehensive, and it appears that they cover commerce, contractual agreements, criminal acts, and fights or altercations. These are general laws needed to operate a large population of individuals in a civilized manner.

Remember the timing here, 2000 BC, a time at the height of the mining in Lake Superior. In this society, it would be probable that you would have freemen, specialized workers. If you were caught stealing food in the daytime, as a bondsman you would get 10 months of bonded labor sentence, and you may find yourself aboard a mining vessels.

Description of Minoan and Aegean Sea Cultures of 2500 BC

A key society and the third culture must be examined, the Minoan culture of the island of Crete. This society came to light in 1900, when Sir Arthur Evans discovered the ruins of Knossos, a one time beautiful city believed to be the capital of a large trading society under a king named Minos. (For the interested reader, the February 1978 issue of National Geographic has done an excellent job of describing its people and their lifestyle).

I would like to break up the description of the Minoan culture into three time periods; the Colonizing Period, the Minos Kingdom Period and the Mycenae Greek period.

The Colonizing Period

There is little to go on here. All that can be said is what must have taken place in order to arrive at the second phase. Neolithic farming and fishing communities existed and were already established on the Island of Crete in 3000 - BC. It can be assumed that early Sumerian traders arrived from the trading city-state of Ugarit to find an ideal concentration point for goods from the Aegean and other points west. Working with the highly qualified local fishermen and sailors, they first would locate a merchant based port where goods could be secured from these local Neolithic villages.

To support this assumption, I would like to quote Michael Wood from his book, *In Search of The Trojan War:*

> At the this time the great age of the Cretan Palaces was begin-ning, a civilization modeled on the Egyptian—Syrian: also at this time the Hurrian civilization (which preceded the Hittite) was developing in Anatolia, strongly influences by the Mesopotamian—Old Assyrian culture with which it had close contacts down the Euphrates valley: Assyrian merchant colonies of considerable size were already established in several places in Anatolia by 1800 BC. In Greece between 1700 and 1600 BC their seems to have been a sudden flowering of Mycenaean civilizations, strongly colored by Cretan elements; this flowering is exemplified in the shaft graves found by Schliemann at Mycenae, dating from the sixteenth century BC. (18) p - 156

I have included the end of the quote about shaft graves, because later we will use this trait to trace this culture west to Ireland and beyond.

The Minos Kingdom Period

Evans was not, however, the first to speak of Crete. For this, I must go to Homer's, *Odyssey*, as quoted by Wood:

> *Out of the wine-dark sea there is a rich and lovely island called Crete, washed by the waves on every side, densely populated with ninety cities . . . one of the ninety cities is a great town called Knossos, and there for nine years King Minos ruled and enjoyed the friendship of almighty Zeus.* (18) p - 94

Another historian, Thucydides, recording the historical traditions of the fifth century wrote, "*Minos was the first person to establish a Navy,*" and "*that he dominated the Aegean and ruled the Cyclades.*" He goes on to say:

> " . . . *In most of which he sent the first colonies, expelling the Cairns and appointing his own sons as governors; and thus did his best to cut down piracy in those waters, a necessary step to secure the revenues for his own use. . . . As soon as Minos had formed his Navy, communications by sea became easier, and he colonized most of the islands.* (18) p - 95

The February 1978 National Geographic Magazine describes the Minoan Culture like this:

> *This was a Bronze Age Culture . . . Minoans flourished on Crete from 3000 BC to 1450 BC . . . Unearthed at the turn of the century, the palace complex at Knossos appears to have been the center of Minoan power and center piece for Europe's first metropolis, which had a population of perhaps 80,000.* (16) p - 144

Frescos were discovered on the walls in this ruin that clearly depict the type of ships these people used, the homes they lived in, and some of the activities in which they participated. Some of these have been photographed and presented here to help clarify to the readers how educated and skilled these people were. They also make the reader aware of this Minoan Culture's love for beauty.

G - 38 Dolphin Fresco, Authors Photo Iraklion Museum, Crete

Also important are the frescos of the ships, for they show us exactly what the culture was using on the water. Some were paddled others were rowed, and some were sailed. The ships that were paddled had from 18 to 23 men per side. These ships appear to have been for royalty or important leaders and rulers. The sailing ships, about the same size, were powered by a large square sail about 6 feet high and 16 feet wide. The sail was hoisted on a single mast with a yardarm on the top and bottom. They were hoisted and held in place by rope or lines almost identical to our modern rope. It is evident that two helmsmen are holding large steering oars. The largest ship shown appears to be powered by paddlers, while at the same time; a large sail is furled and tied down with an alignment parallel with the keel. Several of those ships pictured appear to be about 40 feet long. We can only guess at the width. The fact that these people could trade all over the Mediterranean with these sleek small ships is evident in their records and wares.

G - 39 Replica from Fresco of the ships, Artist (MJ) (16) P - 159

The frescos, also from the Museum on Crete, do not make it apparent when these ships were first developed, but it would have to have been well before the society peeked about 1800 BC.

The Minoan religious symbols are key to the recognition of the spread of the culture. Therefore, I will describe some of them here. Like their mother culture, the Sumerians, the bull remains a key religious symbol to the Minoans. This symbol represents the male sun god Baal. We even find the story of the legendary Gilgamesh in parts of the related Hittite culture. The famous Palace at Knossos is decorated with beautiful paintings and sculptures of bulls.

G - 40 Bull Sculpture, Authors Photo Iraklion Museum, Crete

By the time of the Palace Period in Crete, a religious symbol known as the horns of consecration had already developed. This stylized version of the bull's horns shows how deeply religious the horns of consecration had become.

G - 41 Horns of Consecration, Authors Photo

A second religious symbol, the snake, represented the female Goddess Ishtar. This statue was from the palace at Knossos on Crete.

G 42 Statue of Ishtar & Snakes, Authors Photo

The Mycenae Greek Period

The mainland of Greece was strongly influenced by the Minoan kingdom by 1600 BC. It is apparent that trade and communication existed. According to legend, this relationship had a down side—the Greeks had to send some of their youth in a form of tribute to King Minos.

The Minoan trade empire, as it could be called, is accepted to have been far-reaching:

Westwards the Minoans reached Southern Italy and Sicily . . . and eastward they planted settlements in Rhodes, Kos, Samos and even on the coast of Asia Minor at Iasos and Miletus: The last named gave Minoan traders access to the hinterland of Anatolia. Further afield Minoan merchants dealt with Syria and Egypt, and their ambassadors are portrayed in Egyptian wall paintings: Keftiu (Cretan) ships were evidently a common site in near eastern ports, and the Minoans were the middlemen in the trade westward. A high degree of commercial organization is implied in some of our sources. Texts from Mari on the Euphrates show Cretans as permanent residents at Ugarit - with their interpreters - to buy Elamite tin, which the King of Ugarit supplied. . . . (18) p - 212

The Hittites, for instance, maintained officials at Ugarit to conduct their business, and a 'house of Documents,' a kind of bank, was set up by Ugarit at Hattusas. In Ugarit, finely built chamber tombs have been excavated, suggesting that the Minoan settlers there were people of wealth and sophistication, at ease in a multiracial and multilingual city. (18) p - 212,213

It seems all this wealth was too much for the Mycenae Greeks. They had learned well from the Minoan culture. In about 1420 BC, they occupied Knossos and stepped into the shoes of the Minoan people. They did this, almost completely, in a very short period of time. They had learned the technology well and the basics of trading. However, their war-like nature, coupled with the idea that they could use force to secure new trade areas, was the beginning of the end for peaceful world trade.

"If the Homer catalogue of ships is correct, (a Minoan) King Idomeneus sailed with eighty vessels to help Agamemnon of Mycenae sack Troy." (18) p - 99 This would have been about 1300 BC, before the Dorian Greeks pushed them out of the Aegean.

Although trade still continued for perhaps two hundred years after the takeover, it was based more on power and treaty than on the diplomacy and good will of the previous 1000-year Minoan rule.

The Mycenae Greek time ended just like it started, with force. The Dorian Greeks moved in about 1200 BC. They, in alliance with various rebel northern Hittite kingdoms, pushed some of the Mycenae Greeks, along with the remnants of the trading Minoan and Hittite kingdoms eastward to Cyprus, and southward along the Levant. About 1180 BC, this group attacked Egypt proper in the delta area. Ramses III referred to them as the Sea People. They were in alliance with Egypt's enemy to the west, the Libyans. Ramses III crushed their fleet and resettled them in the vicinity of what is now called Gaza. This was part of the Canaanite culture. Later, these resilient sea-going people will resurface, at which time we will generally refer to them as the Phoenicians. Since the Minoan culture is the key to this work, I would like to present two other views of who these people might really have been. First, let us hear Plato's description of an Aegean culture that might fit.

The Aegean Island of Thera

There exists a theory that is now coming to the forefront concerning the location of Plato's Atlantis. This I mention with regard to the Minoan Culture. I will endeavor to limit my comments to either *"Plato's Dialog,"* words that he attests to as fact or to actual archeological evidence, which we can now support.

Plato describes a great culture that is destroyed and sinks into the sea, presumably because they came into disfavor with the gods. This story has been quoted many times, but I was just made aware of a few new facts when I listened to the A&E Tape called *Atlantis: The Lost Civilization*. Plato was, in fact, writing this second hand in about 400 BC. His source was "Solon," an earlier Greek historian from 594 BC. Now, it seems, Solon had traveled to Egypt to ascertain a more factual early Greek history, since wars and fires had destroyed all their records. This would have been in the time of the rise of the city-states in Greece, known as the Classical Period.

The Egyptians were well aware of the history of the people of the Aegean Sea. They had been trade partners since the early times, about 3000 BC. About 1200 BC, these sea people had attacked Egypt, and then Ramses III crushed them in battle. The Egyptian historians began with a description of a great island culture, one that stretches beyond the Pillars of Hercules, *a culture with a great harbor actually dug into the heart of the city.* This was a culture, no doubt, that was built on trade as most rich island cultures were. Now, stop here and think about this description. Look at the historic map of Thera around the Bronze Age eruption (Circa mid 17th Century BC) and read how the local people describe it now.

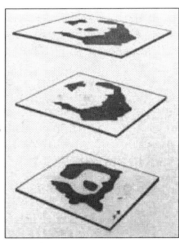

G 43 Island of Thera, Author's Photo Museum on Thera
Ref: photo of wall plaque

"The discovery of fossilized aquatic micro organisms has been interpreted as evidence of the existence of a water filled caldera 18,000 years BP."

Diagram 2: Stages in the formation in the present island group of Thera
    Below: Thera before the late Bronze Age eruption. ***
    Middle: Thera after the late Bronze Age eruption.
    Above: Thera today."

First, Solon was asking about the history of his people, (the Greek people) so surely, it is rational to assume the Great Golden Island City with its great harbor was somewhere near Greece, and that it had been destroyed by an act of God in a day or two. The island of Thera fits this description, but now there is more (it lies beyond the Pillars of Hercules). Did the Egyptians mean the Island Cultural Center or the large trading

Empire? When we try to describe an empire, we talk about its extremities. For example, beyond the Pillars of Hercules would be a good description for the large Minoan trade cartel. After all, the cultural influence of the Minoans has been shown to extend well into Spain and probably on the Tin Isles of Great Britain.

Was Solon actually being told about the Large Aegean Sea Trade Cartel that supplied Ugarit, and therefore, Egypt and Mesopotamia with Copper and Tin for the Bronze Age expansion? Or, did Solon, a trained Historian, get it wrong. I do not think so.

An archeologist, S. Marinatos, has discovered on Thera (Santorini—the modern name), a buried city he called, "Akrotiri." This city fits well into the Minoan culture, as we know it. A fresco portraying the Minoan style bull leaping ceremony was found. The volcanic blast that destroyed Thera took place in approximately 1628 BC. A curious thing was noted, no bodies were found as indicated in Plato's story. Obviously, some warning was available. This does not mean most of the people escaped. However, many probably did rush to the nearest colonies, maybe to Crete, or the Greek mainland. We know the Minoan culture existed after 1628 BC but with a stronger and stronger Mycenae Greek influence. It is highly probable that many of these refugees from the volcanic island had to succumb to their mainland host ideals. This made Crete the only place left in the Aegean Sea with a truly Minoan culture.

Plato says the Atlantian harbor was so busy, that it was a noisy den, day and night, and not a small place. The number—twelve hundred ships from Homer's Trojan War story—seems to fit the picture. The local inhabitants of Santorini say, there is no question, because their grandparents and ancestors have always told them this was Atlantis.

Plato also states of the Atlantians that their greatest value was not their riches, but their virtue. This seems to fit the Minoan's culture in their pre-Mycenae stages—the early priest king era when the colonist trader was careful to honor their new trading partners. It was the time when a few high tech traders could establish a trust with the local Neolithic villagers and secure from them a favorable port site and then proceed to trade. It was a time when they spread the word that the great sun god owned all and when the priest kings were able to use their religions to bring people together for construction of monolithic sites.

If the Solon discussions of Greek history with the Egyptians can be believed, we have a written history telling us about the Minoan trade cartel that actually went into the Atlantic beyond the Pillars of Hercules.

This discussion will stop here because anything beyond would just be conjecture. But, this new archeological information on top of some of the world's oldest written history does raise an interesting question. Is the much-publicized Atlantis culture just a more accurate description of the Minoan trade empire?

Another view and one that gives much of the new current insight on the Old European Culture is discussed below.

The Goddess View / the Old European Culture

For a somewhat different view of how the Minoan culture got started and functioned, we need to read Rinae Eisler's book entitled, *The Chalice and the Blade.* Here, she does a much better job than I, to create a sense of who the early Neolithic people were, and whom we find on Crete prior to 2500 BC.

She tells about the early Neolithic settlements, *"The towns of Catal Huyuk and Hacilar. They were found in what used to be called the plains of Anatolia, now Modern Turkey"* . . . *"The man who directed these excavations for the British Institute of Archaeology at Ankara, was James Mellaart"* (15) p7.

She goes on to point out that a Goddess based society existed from Jericho in the south, into Tell-es-sawwan on the Tigris River and up into the Annotation Peninsula at Catal Huyuk and west to Hacilar. This society continued from about 7000 BC up until it collapsed about 1200 BC with the final fall of Crete.

> *Although this is not generally brought out, the numerous Neolithic excavations that yield Goddess figurines and symbols span a wide geological area going far beyond the Near and Middle East. As far east as Harppa and Mohenjo-Daro in India, large numbers of terra-cotta female figurines had earlier been found. . . . Goddess figurines have also been found in European sites as far west as those of the so-called megalithic cultures who built the huge, carefully engineered stone monuments at Stonehenge and Amesbury in England.* (15) p-8
>
> *Some of the most vivid evidence of this geocentric artistic tradition comes to us from Mallard's excavations of Catal Huyuk. . . . this digging alone uncovered a period spanning approximately eight hundred years, from about 6500 to about 5700 B.C.E. and what we find here is a remarkable advanced center of art, with wall paintings, plaster relief, stone sculpture, and large quantities of Goddess figurines made of clay, . . .* (15) p-11.

She quotes Mellaart as he describes, *"The birth of architecture and conscious planning: its economy to advanced practices in agriculture and stockbreeding; and its numerous imports to a flourishing trade in raw materials."*

> *In fact, by circa 6000 B.C.E., not only was the agricultural revolution an established fact, but—to quote Mellaart—"fully agricultural societies began expanding into hitherto marginal territories. . . . some of this contact, as in Crete and Cyprus, definitely went by sea.* (15) p-11

She goes on to quote Gimbutas:

> Wheat, barley, vetch, pea, and other legumes were cultivated, and all the domesticated animals present in the Balkans today, except for the horse, were bred. Pottery technology and bone-and stone-working techniques had advanced, and copper metallurgy was introduced into east central Europe by 5500 B.C.E. . . . The use of sailing boats is attested from the sixth millennia onwards by their incised depictions on ceramics. (15) p 13

MS. Eisler goes on to tell about the art and symbols being used. The bulls, serpents, and butterflies are all present. The butterflies and the snakes are a positive representation of metamorphous or rebirth of all the mother goddess blessings. The bull's horns are horns of consecration. The double ax is present but not explained.

> *The story of Cretan civilization begins around 6000 B.C.E., when a small colony of immigrants, probably from Anatolia, first arrived on the island's shores. It was they who brought the Goddess with them, as well as an agrarian technology that classifies these first settlers as Neolithic. For the next four thousand years there was slow and steady technological progress, in pottery making, weaving, metallurgy, engraving, architecture, and other crafts, as well as increasing trade and the gradual evolution of the lively and joyful artistic style so characteristic of Crete. Then approximately 2000 B.C.E., Crete entered what archaeologists call the Middle Minoan or Old Palace period.*
>
> *This was already well into the Bronze Age, a time when in the rest of the then civilized world the Goddess was steadily being displaced by war like male gods. She was still revered—as Hathor and Isis in Egypt, as Astarte or Ishtar in Babylon, or as the sun Goddess of Arinna in Anatolia. But it was now only as a secondary deity, described as the consort or mother of more powerful male gods. For this was increasingly a world where the*

*power of women was also on the decline, a world where male
dominance and wars of conquest and counter conquest were
everywhere becoming the norm.*

*In the island of Crete where the Goddess was still supreme,
there are no signs of war. Here the economy prospered and the
arts flourished. And even when in the fifteenth century BCE the
island finally came under Achaean dominion—when
archaeologists no longer speak of Minoan but rather Minoan-
Mycenaean culture—the Goddess and the way of thinking and
living she symbolized still appeared to have held fast.* (15) p-
30,31.

*Knossos, which may have had a hundred thousand inhabitants,
was connected to the south coast ports by a fine paved highway,
the first of its kind in Europe. Its streets, like those of other palace
centers such as Mallia and Phaistos, were paved and drained,
fronted with neat two or three story houses, flat roofed and
sometimes with a penthouse for use on hot summer nights.* (15) p-
34.

Another scholar, Reynold Higgins, sums up this aspect of Cretan life
as follows:

*Religion for the Cretans was a happy affair, and was
celebrated in palace-shrines, or else in open-air sanctuaries on
the tops of mountains and in sacred caves. . . . Their religion was
closely bound up with their recreation. First in importance were
the bull-sports, which probably took place in the central courts of
palaces. Young men and women working in teams would take it in
turns to grasp the horn of a charging bull and somersault over its
back.* (15) p-35.

*Even among the ruling classes personal ambition seems to
have been unknown; nowhere do we find the name of an author
attached to a work of art nor a record of the deeds of a ruler.* (15)
p-36

*A remarkable feature of Cretan culture is that there are no
statues or reliefs of those who sat on the thrones of Knossos or of
any of the palaces.* (15) p-37

This description seems to fit many of the recent articles and
information on the Minoan culture of Crete. It is obvious that the
"thought process of the Minoans" held concepts that allowed for peaceful
coexistence. I believe this was the essential ingredient that allowed for

the one-thousand-year period of mining on Lake Superior, while the rest of the world struggled with each other over the riches produced earlier. It saddens me to think what our level of society could have been, if we had been cooperating instead of fighting from 2000 BC to the present.

It is obvious that prior to 2500 BC Crete was comprised of a creative mixture of the Old Neolithic values along with the more modern urban technologies. These may, or may not, have been learned from the urban center of Ugarit where the "Highbred Vigor" of mixing cultures existed. Regardless of how it happened, that was the situation that set up the biggest mining boom anywhere in the world up until that time, and for probably, a thousand years after it.

The Levant

Other Canaanite cultures had a significant bearing on the regional trade, and we will describe them, briefly. The Early Bronze, "EB" Age, in the southern Levant, spans the millennium roughly between 3300 BC and 2300 BC. Conveniently, it is divided into EB I, II or III with additional final phases that differ from all the preceding phases. The earliest phase, EB I (3300 to 3050BC), was by characterized by farming villages. Few sites reached any size with one exception, Arad.

It was only in EB II (c. 3050 BC to 2700 BC) that the urbanism became a significant factor in the society. This coincides with the emergence of the fully literate urban societies of Sumer in southern Mesopotamia and the early Egyptian dynasties. The trade between these powers was growing. Many settlements in the Levant were well located to take advantage of the land route along which trade caravans traveled.

During a period of wars and chaos many of these city-states along the Levant were destroyed and abandoned, but later as the populations stabilized things improved.

> *Cities were once again built in the middle of the bronze age (c. 2000-1550 BC), some of them on top of the abandoned remains of earlier ones. Traditions of urbanism were obviously preserved during the intervening nomadic era, perhaps in the cities of the northern coast, such as Ras Shamra"* [Ugarit—my words] *"and Biblos. As is apparent from the archaeological record, these cities continued as large-scale and prosperous settlements with no interruptions.* (19) p- 50

> *Together with renewed prosperity went a great increase in population. The period was also one of continued technological developments.* (19) p- 50

An independent Canaanite culture flourished in the early 2nd millennium BC. . . . The Phoenicians were culturally the heirs of these Bronze Age Canaanite craftsmen. (19) p 51.

Their center was at Avaris (Tell Dhaba) where archaeologists have excavated a palatial structure and found evidence for a material culture that is characteristically Canaanite, as well as remarkably Minoan-style frescos. (19) p- 51

The Gods of Canaan

Baal, the Sun God, was represented by a young man with an upright arm holding a shaft of lighting or thunder. Alternately, he was represented as a bull. He was usually worshipped outside on a "Bamot," (a high place or open air altar). The female goddess was Astarte or Asherah, the sacred tree, the tree of life, nourishing and fertile.

The texts on Canaanite Deities were not discovered until 1929 at Ugarit. They were recorded in characters rather like cruciform but used as an alphabet system. It is obvious the early Canaanite culture in Ugarit had a lot of similarities to the Minoan culture of King Minos of Crete:

1. They worshipped the Sun God, Baal, often represented as a Bull.

2. They used a similar, if not the same, linear A script.

3. They were a strong shipping and trading culture, well connected in the major urban centers of the time.

This city, (Ugarit) the capital of the fertile kingdom, was at the center of a far-flung trade network, and was a rich and cosmopolitan place. (19) p - 54

About 380 letters, or parts of letters, on clay tablets have been found at Te el-Amarna. They were mostly written in Akkadian, which was the Semitic language of Mesopotamia, and used as the international language of diplomacy throughout the Near East at the time. (19) p - 55

Other Related Cultures

Other similar cultures developed east from Sumer, which seem to be related. These cultures lead one to believe the Sumerian urban center was, in effect, colonizing for trade both east and west.

The Indus Valley Cultures

One similar and possibly related culture built two cities, Harppa and Mohenjo-daro, in the Indus river valley.

The single most important feature of the cities is the planning and control evident even in the oldest levels. There is no indication of random growth. Instead, the Indus cities were apparently built with all their mature features present in the beginning and then as remarkably, were preserved with little observable change for almost a thousand years.

These Indus valley cities were built around 2500 BC by a culture already skilled enough to create a city three miles around, laid out on a rectangle street pattern, and with a well at each house. Each house also had a bath and latrine some even with seats. The drain system was made of brick and was covered. The early activity in this valley also goes back to 3000 BC. (13) p – 3, 10*

This culture can be associated to the Minoan Culture by the following similarities:

1. They both were trading societies.
2. They both were quite secure in that they did not develop serious fortifications.
3. They both practiced an unusual sort of cult or manhood ritual, where the man laid down in front of a bull, and then jumped up and swung over his horns.
4. Both societies became established around 2500 BC and ceased to function about 1450 BC. They did not cease to exist. They just experienced a very significant change, just as though the strong central government that had served them for a thousand years was destroyed.

Dilman (Bahrain)

A third island city that fit the same time period and may fit in other ways was known as Dilman. This island state was known to trade with cities in the Indus valley and Ur in Mesopotamia. Although the ship's logs and trader's books do not mention Crete or Cyprus in the reference that I found, they were closely related in the trade they carried on and the products handled. *"The Dilman trade was taking place 2450 BC to 1794*

BC and, probably before and after those dates," according to an article by Ali Akbar H. Bushiri of Bahrain. (14)

It is not my aim to teach anyone about intricacies of these cultures, but there is one more point you need to know. These cultures, at least the Minoan of Crete and the unknown people of the Indus valley, were probably not Caucasian or Aryan. *"Early Aryan hymns express disdain for these early people of the Indus Valley. They describe these non-Aryans as dark and snub-nosed."* (13) p-3

Cultures That Did Not Yet Exist

As part of our proof, I would like to digress here to make a point about some cultures, which had not yet begun to emerge prior to 2500 BC. If a culture did not exist during the entire 2400 BC to 1200 BC window, we could say they had an alibi and could not have been the ancient miners. I have listed the accepted date these cultures first came on the scene.

You may be surprised that I have included the Mycenae Greeks, the Celts, and the Olmec since they are listed as part of the trading people at the end of the period. The reason is simple. These cultures are in one way an effect of the trade, instead of the cause of it. For this reason they can not be considered a part of the causal culture.

First Dates for These Cultures		
Europe	*North America*	*Central America*
Roman 500 BC	*Adena Mound Builders 1000 BC*	*Mayan 1530 BC*
Mycenae Greek 1650 BC	*Hopewell Mound Builders 150 BC*	*Olmec 1500 BC*
Celtic 1200 BC	*Mississippian Mound Builders 700 AD*	

Summary of Possible Cultures

Of the three cultures that fit the time line, Egyptian, Sumerian, and the Cypriot / Minoan / Ugarit trading city-states, we already have one very strong candidate. It is the trading city-states.

Egypt, although a trading partner, was not a primary contender because they would have given away the direct involvement in their extensive historical record. The Old Sumerian culture, although the probable source of the demand, had been driven out of its home-land by 1800 BC, yet the trade had continued. This leaves the Cypriot / Minoan / Ugarit city-states as the most logical contenders. The evidence of the Canaanite gods Baal, (the Bull) and Ishtar (the snake) and the well documented involvement in the copper trade also points to the city-states. For this reason, we will look closely at this culture in the section on Motive and Ability, Chapter 5.

We have also added a time line on the next page to make the associations more clear.

G - 44 Time Line

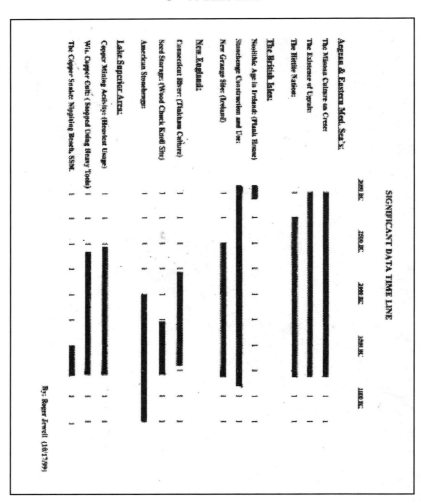

5 *Motive and Ability*

Whenever any large undertaking happens, it is always easy to see someone with a motive. Those in our industrial production sector all study motive or motivation. It is the essence of how to create through the use of others. By others, we normally mean any large group.

Old Copper Culture

As stated earlier, we have not been able to find a suitable motive for the hunter/gatherer Old Copper Complex natives of Northern Wisconsin to mine large amounts of copper ore, if they were acting alone. Yet the evidence is there. These people were, in all probability, involved in the mining of this copper. So a motive must have existed and it had to be a very significant one.

The motive had to justify the change in lifestyle the mining would necessitate. Trade or new technologies are the usual route a society takes before this can happen. More efficient hunting tools, better fishing equipment, and more efficient transportation might make the change possible. In fact, at the beginning of the early woodland phase of Native American culture, such changes were happening. Just to mention a few, the bow and arrow, fishnets, canoes, pottery, and cultivation all came along around this time. Thor Conway, in his book, *Archaeology in Northeastern Ontario, Searching for our Past,* states, *"Bows and Arrows (were) introduced around 1600 BC"* on the northeast shore of Lake Superior.

To establish a motive and provide the window of opportunity for our old copper culture, we must assume a trade in these new products and technologies existed. Without such trade, it would not have been possible for a culture to stop what it was doing and start mining copper, which is evidently what they did. The only thing these tribes would have had to trade would be their labor and maybe a few furs.

A Trade Partner Motive and Ability

Who had the motive to remove the copper from the region? This is a question we have already addressed in a number of ways. Obviously, the Mediterranean cultures were actively trading for copper at that time. However, did these cultures have the ability to set up a trade network that would travel many thousand miles around the world in search of copper or other metals? We will consider this question now. We will see these cultures not only had the motive, but definitely, the skill to pull it off.

We have one primary culture and one subculture on the scene at the proper time. They are the Minoan/Cypriot/Ugarit trading cartel. From now on, I will call them the "Minoans." There is also very sketchy evidence of a group known as the Red Paint People, or the Archaic Marine Group on this side of the Atlantic.

Since we have little to go on to treat the Marine Archaic as a culture, we can only say this: They were a sea going people. It appears they lived mainly on fish. In fact, in Ohio, there was a group who were called the Fish-Eaters. They also used red ochre. They were the precursors to the first mound people. The Red Paint People, as I would prefer to call them, were capable of ocean travel. There were swordfish parts in their midden piles. They set up their camps on mountain tops, some say for the beauty, because they always overlooked the lakes, rivers, or seas. I think this may have been for more practical reasons. They could watch for the approach of friends or enemies alike. There are standing stones, and other stone monuments found in their associations. Most of what I could find on this culture, came from a recent "special," aired in 1994 on public TV. However, acting alone this group doesn't seam to have a motive.

The Minoans are better known. I don't think anyone would question that a group that could build elaborate palaces and artwork had the technical ability to do the mining. The question always goes back to this: Could this group provide the logistics to mine the copper? By this, we mean, did they have the men, money, and machinery (ships) to do the job?

Recently, archeologists have discovered some shipwrecks that make it quite clear what the abilities of this trading cartel were.

The Minoan Ability

The Age of Sail

> *The oldest ship of which there is definite knowledge was built for the funeral of the Pharaoh, Cheops (3960 - 3908 BC). Found in his tomb in a trench and covered with sand. This ship was an open-hulled vessel (it had no deck), 40 m (133 ft.) in length, with a maximum beam of 8 m (26 ft). It was constructed of about 600 separate pieces of wood, the largest being 23 m (75 ft) long.*
> *The Phoenicians, who ruled the Mediterranean shores from about 1000 BC to 250 BC, improved on the Egyptian design.*

They built a similar vessel of approximately 100 feet in length, with which to trade on the Mediterranean, and larger Tarshish ships with which they ventured out through the Straits of Gibraltar, up to the Sicily Isles. And, if Herodotus is to be believed, around the Cape of Good Hope into the Indian Ocean. (25) Age of sail

Ancient Egyptian carvings reveal that the stones used to build the pyramids were transported by boat. Egyptian wall painters and pottery makers depicted sail and paddle boats on their ceramics. By perhaps 3000 BC, Egyptian sailors were voyaging as far as Crete, a round trip of about 950 km (about 600 miles). They brought back cedar wood, for Egypt even then possessed few trees from which to construct boats. Egyptian nautical development occurred along with the invention of woven cloth for sails and twisted rope for rigging. A modern sailor, looking at rope made thousands of years ago and preserved in the dry air of the pharaohs ' tombs, might well be amazed to realize that this ancient rope is constructed in a way still used today—three strands in a right hand twist. (25) Age of Sail.

Egyptians moved multi-ton blocks by ship, which they used to build the pyramids. Empirical evidence leads us to believe the stones of Stonehenge were also moved on a ship. Both of these activities predate the copper mining era. It is safe to say, ships of at least 100 feet long were in use by the culture we are still considering. Since none of the pieces of ore would be expected to outweigh these huge stones, it would have been unlikely they would have had a problem.

The Ship Wreck Of Ulu Burun: In 1982, a sponge diver located a shipwreck off the coast of Turkey at the promontory of Ulu Burun. Since its discovery, this has been considered one of the most important shipwrecks ever found. It has been dated to about the 14th century BC. This puts it well before the end of the period we are concerned with. The vessel was about 50 feet long and was made of wooden hull planks held together with mortis-and-tenon joints. Of key importance to this study was the cargo. Here, I would like to quote the National Geographic writer, George F. Bass:

" . . . *as we carefully surveyed the site, we found that the ships principal cargo had been copper ingots. There were about 200 of them—more than six times the number we had found at Cape Gelidonya. Each of the ingots weighs around 60 pounds, the equivalent of an ancient talent. (24) p - 709*

This entire article is must reading for any one interested in the historic trade of this period. One key piece of information secured from the Ulu Burun wreck was the assurance of accuracy in Homers two stories, The Odyssey and The Iliad. We all realize, no matter if a work is fiction or legend, the audience must relate to it. Consequently, the descriptions must be accurate and understandable. Yet in this wreck, there were actual mortis and tendon joints holding the two-inch by ten-inch planks together. They were also pinned with hard wood pins, which match the story perfectly. I want to digress here for a moment to discuss Homer.

We know now that Homer and the Trojan Wars do represent reality. This has been proven by the German researcher, H. Schliemann and others. We are also beginning to realize the Mycenae Greek period; roughly 1450 BC to 1200 BC represents the end of the Minoan period. At this time, the Minoan culture (the Phaeacians or Phoenicians) was the master of the seas, blessed by the gods, and the Greeks were the students. So when the Goddess, Calypso, gave things to Odysseus, she gave him the best—the tools and the materials of the masters. I want you to read the direct quote of how Odysseus built his boat.

> *First she gave him a great axe of bronze. Its double blade was sharpened well, and the shapely handle of olive wood fixed firmly in its head was fitted to his grip. Next she handed him an adz of polished metal; and then led the way for him to the farthest part of the island, where the trees grew tall. . . . Presently Calypso brought him augers. With these he drilled through all his planks, cut them to fit each across each other, and fixed this flooring together by means of dowels driven through the interlocking joints, giving the same width to his boat as a skilled shipwright would choose in designing the hull for a broad bottomed trading vessel. He next put up the decking, which he fitted to the ribs at short intervals, finishing off with long gunwales down the sides. . . . Meanwhile the goddess Calypso had brought him cloth with which to make the sail. This he manufactured too; and then lashed the braces, halyards, and sheets in their places on board. Finally he dragged her down on rollers into the tranquil sea.* (27) p - 94

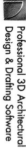

Chief Architect®

Professional 3D Architectural Design & Drafting Software

Please send me my FREE Trial Version!

Name:

Company:

Street:

City:

State/ZIP:

Email:

FHB09/08

Call Today for your
Free Trial Version!
or Download Now

800-482-4433
www.chiefarchitect.com
sales@chiefarchitect.com

Chief Architect, Inc.
6500 N. Mineral Dr.
Coeur d'Alene, ID 83815

PLACE
STAMP
HERE

G - 45 Bronze Minoan Axe From Crete, Necklace Item

Iraklion Museum Crete

Homer, in The Iliad, describes King Agamemnon's preparations for battle. On numerous occasions, he describes fleets of hollow ships and fleets of black ships. These fleets commonly represent 30, 40, or 50 ships, and there are many fleets. At this time the Greek structure was city-states. The king of each city-state sent a fleet. There are two important points here to be noted. First, the fleet sizes of 40 or 50 ships were common. Second, the term, hollow ships, implied a top deck. So again we have a description from a legitimate source of solid wood ships completely decked over.

For the sake of this work, it is enough to know there were little 50-foot long ships sailing between Crete and possibly Egypt carrying 12,000 pounds of pure copper ingots. . . . *"Enough when mixed with tin to manufacture a total of 300 bronze helmets, 300 bronze corsets, 3000 spearheads, and 3000 bronze swords!"* (24) p – 719,720

This craft had a mixed cargo from many nations. A large number of Canaanite and Mycenaean artifacts were aboard. It is apparent, from this one wreck; a varied trade existed consisting of the primary items of value for all the existing cultures of the region.

G - 46 Copper Ingot, Author's Photo, British Museum

We know the Minoan Cartel, and probably any other good-sized kingdom of the developed world at that time, had the technology to ship multi-ton loads of ore. Let's look for some quotations actually written during this period for the purpose of documenting it.

The Dilmun Trade to the Sumerian City of Ur: My first quotations are from tablets found in Ur. They are in relation to shipping from the east on the Persian Gulf. Remember, as I pointed out earlier, the trade went both east and west from the Fertile Crescent. The technology and trading format would be similar either way. However, the dry hot air helped to do a better job of preserving the actual manuscripts in the east.

The quotes are from an article by Ali-Akbar H. Bushiri, of Bahrain. *"Even in those most ancient days ca. 6000 BC, men were sailing from various ports, over open water. . . ."* The information provided by the economic texts on Mesopotamian tablets and also inferred from the seal stones from Dilmun, support this level of trade. One 1900 BC shipment of copper weighed eighteen and a half metric tons. The following quotes will show more detail. (23) p - 207

> Tablet No.7: *"This tablet is dated to Gutians "Gudea", the king of the city of Lagash, BC 2050, . . . Timber, Marble, Bronze and Gold are brought from the surrounding areas for the building of the temple . . . ." (23)*
>
> Tablet No. 9: *"A tablet from the city of Ur dated 1794 BC Lu-Meshlam-Tae and Nifsisanabsa have borrowed from Ur-Ninmar, 2 minas of silver, 5 kur of sesame-oil, 30 garnets as capital for a partnership for an expedition to Dilmun to buy copper there." (23)*
>
> Tablet No.11: *"A receipt tablet dated to 2027 BC from Ur. Ur-gur, the captain of a large boat, for ten talents of different kinds of wool of ordinary quality, put in a boat to Dilmun." (23)*
>
> Tablet No. 13: *"A receipt tablet issued by Lu-Endilla for goods received from the temple of Nannar, the principal temple in the city of Ur, dated between 2026 and 2024 BC. Sixty talents of wool, seventy garments, one hundred and eighty skins, six hur of good sesame-oil, as merchandise for buying copper." (23)*

The following tablet indicates the type of moral code these traders followed. It was based on trust and a system of measures that was known to all. Items were often listed by quality, for example: *"good Sesame oil."* There were disagreements as the following tablet indicated.

> Tablet No. 15: *"A letter from one Nanni to a Dilmunian Trader in copper in Ur under the name of Ea-Nasir, dated between 1813 to 1790 BC."* "When you came, you said, 'I will give ingots to Gimil-Sin.' That's what you said, but you have not done so; you offer bad ingots to my messenger, saying, 'take it or leave it'. Who

am I that you should treat me so contemptuously? Are we not both gentlemen? . . . Who is there among Dilmun traders who has acted against me in this way?" (23)

There was an interesting sidelight found in these tablets. The system of weights used at Dilmun was the Mina. It was related to a system used along the Indus River instead of Ur. The Mina equaled very closely to 1,375 grams, 48 ounces (3 pounds). The stone weights weighed: 685 grams (24 ounces), 370 grams (13 ounces), probably 12 ounces, 170 grams (6 ounces), 27 grams (1.0 ounces), 13.5 grams (0.5ounces) and 1.7 grams (06 ounces), probable .05 ounces.

The author finds it unusual that this system of weights differs from Ur. But I think further investigation will show that Sargon, the Semitic king, had already displaced the Old Sumerian language and system of weights by this time. You might find this system if you go to Crete or the Anatolian Peninsula where the early Sumerian influence to the west may have lasted longer.

I am struck by how well the Dilmun Mina fits into the pound and ounce system. We can tell by the size of the weights and the products listed that gold and silver was already being used as a medium of exchange. We would say money, but again, I digress. I just find it so interesting that these people, who we often think of as just above stoneage, had such a well-developed system of writing for contracts, used money for a medium of exchange, and that their weight system seems to fit exactly into ours. In fact, we could learn from the brevity of these contracts.

G - 47 Contract & Loan Agreement, Authors Photo

Although this next story took place around 1150 BC or 1200 BC, after the heyday of Egypt and Levant trade had passed, the words make it quite clear how the economics of international trade worked in that earlier time.

The Egyptian Pharaoh would send an emissary (messenger) up to Sidon, Byblos, or Ugarit, probably with a gift as partial payment in advance. The gift would be silver or other items worthy of the requested contract. I am sure it was well understood. A set percentage, paid in advance, was required to commission a contract work or trade. When the work was completed, the emissary would return with the payment of so many shiploads of grain or fabrics of Egyptian production.

Journey of Wen-Amon to Phoenicia

To begin with, you must know this is based on a direct translation from a papyrus now in the Moscow Museum, which comes from El-Hibeh in Middle Egypt and dates to the early twenty-first Dynasty (11th century BC). Wen-Amon was sent from Egypt up to the Levant to secure logs for some ships. On the way there, the silver he was to give the prince was stolen. It was at the waning point in Egyptian power. Therefore, he no longer commanded the respect previously bestowed upon him. When I pick up the story, he is in a discussion with the prince in charge of the city of Byblos.

> *But I said to him, "wasn't it an Egyptian ship? Now it is Egyptian crews, which sail under Ne-su-ba-neb-Ded! He has no Syrian crews." And he said to me: "Aren't there twenty ships here in my harbor which are commercial relations with Ne-su-Ba-neb-Ded? As to this Sidon, the other (place) which you have passed, aren't there fifty more ships there which are commercial relations with Werket-El, and which are drawn up to his house?" And I was silent in this great time.* (20) p - 19

Wen-Amon continues to argue with the prince for help in securing the logs.

> *"Your father did (it), (5) your grandfather did (it), and you will do it too!" So I spoke to him. But he said to me: "To be sure they did it! And if you give me (something) for doing it, I will do it! Why, when my people carried out this commission, Pharaoh—life, prosperity, health!—sent six ships loaded with Egyptian goods, and they unloaded them into their storehouses! You—what is it that you're bringing me—me also?"*

So he said to me: "If the ruler of Egypt were the lord of mine, and I were his servant also, he would not have to send me silver and gold, saying: Carry out the commission of Amon!' There would be no carrying of a royal-gift, such as they used to do for my father. As for me—me also--I am not your servant! (20) p - 20

This sounds all very familiar today. It was simply government-backed international trade. The Egyptians even owned warehouses in Byblos from which the items were turned over to the prince to distribute to his merchantmen for securing the contracted items—always with a little extra for the prince, I suppose.

Smaller or regularly scheduled trade runs were probably made weekly or monthly. As a shipload of copper came in, the grain and fabric were probably traded on the spot from the Egyptian warehouses. This would provide more efficient use of the ships.

It was a good system that worked well as long as there was peace and trust between the kingdoms and, at the same time, adequate control over the seas. It did, in fact, work for about a thousand years. These port cities would always have warehouses of goods ready to trade belonging either to the Pharaoh or the merchant king or one of his "commercial relations." This might have been another name for a sanctioned merchant of the kingdom. These trade goods would be sent out to a more distant kingdom, such as King Minos at Crete on the Aegean Sea. King Minos would reach further out to secure the raw materials of his trade. It is the extent of these trade connections that I believe we have long underestimated.

But let us return to our story. The Byblos prince is now speaking: *"If I cry out to the Lebanon, the heavens open up and the logs are here on the shore of the sea!"* The prince goes on in a rather bragging challenging fashion and ends saying, *"What are these silly trips they have you make."* Wen-Amon goes on to say,

And I say to him: "(That's) not true! What I am on are no 'silly trips' at all! There is no ship upon the River, which does not belong to Amon! The sea is his, and the Lebanon is his, of which you say: 'It is mine!' It forms the nursery for User-het- Amon, the lord of (every) ship!"

He goes on to point out that Amon is God of all and also life and health, sort of a veiled threat to the stubborn prince. The argument worked, probably, because Egypt could still reach out and make it hard for a city-state as close as Byblos, with only twenty ships.

So, the prince of Byblos loads up a few bow posts and four timbers, and sends them back to Egypt with his own emissary. Here again, we pick up the story:

> *And in the first month of the second season his messenger who had gone to Egypt came back to me in Syria. And Ne-su-Ba-neb-Ded and Ta-net-Amon sent: 4 Jars and 1 kak-men of gold; 5 jars of silver; 10 pieces of clothing in royal linen; 10 kherd of good Upper Egyptian Linen; 500 (rolls of) finished papyrus; 500 cow hides; 500 ropes; 20 sacks of lentils; and 30 baskets of fish.*
>
> *And the Prince was glad, and he detailed three hundred men and three hundred cattle and he put supervisors at their head, to have them cut down the timber.* (20) p - 21

The Egyptian, Wen-Amon, finally gets his logs and starts for home. A fleet of eleven ships, from a different land, challenges him once more, but he dissuades them and his ships finally reach home in Egypt. It was such a hair-raising event that he has it officially recorded.

A lot can be inferred from this 3000-year-old story. The prince of a port like Byblos could take a commission (contract) to secure raw materials like timber or copper, both of which were not really available to Egypt. He had only twenty ships, so it would be unlikely he would send more than 3 or 4 of them on a very long voyage to Spain or England. Some of the larger ports, like Sidon, had larger fleets of about 50 ships. Fleets like the one that detained him could easily have 10 ships. This one had eleven.

The Size of Ships and Fleets

We learn from Homer's story that Crete provided about 80 ships for the battle of Troy. From this, we can assume the Minoan kings probably had a lot more ships under his command, maybe as many as two hundred or more. This would make it possible to send out fleets of 5 or 10 ships on very long trips to carry out a "commission" and two or three years may have been common.

The exact size of these ships is unknown. However, we can estimate sizes from several different locations.

1. An actual Egyptian ship was found in Pharaoh Cheop's tomb (3960-3908 BC). It was 133 feet long and 26 feet wide. It was made of planks using mortis and tendon construction techniques.

It did not have the deck covered, but this was probably a design choice for the tomb ship. I do not think it can be implied all decks were open to the weather. Egyptian ships and barges were used to move very large multi-ton stones so this size was probably common.

2. The 34-century-old merchantman trade ship, found off an Asia Minor coast promontory called Ulu Burun, was my second example. It was about 50 feet long. The width was not estimated, but it was probably at least 10 to 12 feet if we use today's ships as a standard. This ship was carrying 12,000 pounds of copper and other incidental cargo.

3. The pictures on the Minoan walls, uncovered by Evans, give a third size estimate. These frescos show both pleasure craft and cargo vessels. By attributing a 6-foot scale to the men on the ships, the merchant ship scaled off at about 40 feet, and the larger passenger carrying vessels scaled off at about 50 feet. The passenger carrying ships had as many as 21 paddlers. This would imply a crew of about 42 plus the captain, maybe, as many as fifty. The drawing show what looks like about 10 to 15 seated royal or official passengers.

These lengths match the fifty-foot sunken ship off Ulu Burun very well. This is also in line with the technology of a singletree keel and a singletree mast. These would make very strong little ships, if properly decked. Yet, it would be small enough to handle with 30 or 40 good men on ropes. It would also be small enough to get into shallow protected bays to conduct trades in remote lands.

Although a much later ship, about 900 AD, the Viking ship *Gokstad* is well documented. It gives us a good estimate of the probable dimension of a singletree mast ship.

This ship is just over 76 feet long and the maximum width is 17 feet; the height from the bottom of the keel to the gunwale amidships is seven feet. The weight of the hull fully equipped is estimated at 20 tons. It contains a strong "mast fish" and 16 pairs of ores. It is a strong ship, because it was built on a solid keel, which has been taken from a single oak tree, which may have been about 80 feet high. (26) p - 9,10

The larger ships of 100 feet plus were probably technically possible, but their widespread use was, in my opinion, unlikely. Even in modern times, the 80 to 100 foot length was quite common for wooden sailing vessels.

I think we can safely assume that the fleets were made up of sturdy little 50 to 100 foot single sail merchant ships. These ships could easily carry from 10,000 to 20,000 pounds of copper each since the loads were probably mixed in most cases—maybe furs and copper coming into the urban centers. Cloth, garments, dyes, beads, and copper tools were shipped out.

The inventory on board the Egyptian ship designed to pay for the lumber in our earlier story, was filled with a quite diverse cargo. The "Ulu Burun" ship was also handling a quite diverse cargo. These ships handled the commerce of the day. It would just be more efficient to mix bulk loads with high-density loads, thereby avoiding the hauling of a lot of waste ballast rock.

In fact, Michael Wood states in his book, *In Search Of The Trojan War*: *"A Greek marauder in Lycia in around 1420 BC presented a threat to a Hittite army with a force of 100 chariots and perhaps 1000 troops; A rich city like Ugarit could man 150 ships (with mercenaries) for an offensive campaign—perhaps 7000 fighting men."(18) p - 159* These city-states were quite opulent by this time, and shipping was their game.

Now, let's go back to the problem at hand. Could they move the 20 to 50 million pounds of copper removed from Lake Superior? The answer is simply, yes, easily. Twenty million pounds divided by 400 years equals 50,000 pounds per year. A small fleet of three to five ships, making a round trip every three years or so, would be just about ideal. This would be a nice little side venture for a Minoan merchant king with good connections in Britain or Ireland and a fleet of 40 or 50 ships.

G – 48 Author's sketch of Minoan Merchant Ship

Interesting Circumstantial Evidence, Fire Signals

I have inserted a small bit on fire signals, a system that natives were using in North America when the white men arrived. Apparently, it was also being used in the Middle East at a very early time. A quote from the letters of "Mari," written about 1730 to 1700 BC at ancient Mari on the Middle Euphrates:

> To my lord say: Thus Bannum, thy servant. Yesterday, (5) I departed from Mari, and spent the night at Zuruban. All the Benjaminites (15) raised fire-signals (note) from Samanum to Ilurm-Muluk, from Ilum-Muluk to Mishlan, all the cities of the Benjaminites of the Terqa district raised fire signals in response, and so far I have not ascertained the meaning of those signals. Now, I shall determine the meaning and I shall write to my lord whither it is thus or not. Let the guard of the city of Mari be strengthen, and let my lord not go outside the gate. (20) p - 260

With the use of fire signals, the ancients were able to communicate with great rapidity over considerable distances. The use of these fire symbols may point out a second use for hills and promontories. Maybe, the traders were using hills for rapid communication—sort of a *smoke-a-phone*. In fact, these hilltop locations may have aided night crossings made over dangerous waters. The use of lighthouses was already in practice by this time.

This completes our section on Ability. I think it would only be American bias to think these cultures could not ship copper across the Atlantic Ocean, especially, if they island jumped across the north end of the Atlantic.

6 *The People*

It is apparent that I must adequately describe this group of Minoan/Cypriot/Canaanite traders in a more distinct fashion, if the reader is to follow their journey through time and space. I will start with a time frame and develop the description from the most important archeological records that I have discovered in my study.

3800 BC: At this time the most distinct culture, we have showing the traits of our people, has been named "Sumerian." It was the primary culture in the southern end of Mesopotamia. Here we must be very careful to point out, that we are talking about the people who spoke the Old Sumerian language. *"The southern part of the plain also became known as Sumer."* (17) p-20

This area was taken over by its Semitic elements by 2000 BC. "However, recently, a reassessment of the astronomical evidence favors the date 1848 BC." (30) p - 20

Therefore, when we speak of Sumerians, we are speaking of the culture in southern Mesopotamia, during the period from 3800 BC to 1800 BC. The focal center was the cities of Uruk, Lagash, and Ur and the surrounding areas. This is extremely important to remember since out of this culture flowed the trading merchant families we will talk about in the rest of this book. They colonized both east and west from this base.

Physical Characteristics

Sumerian body type and description: *"We call the civilization Sumerian after inscriptions which refer to the kings of Sumer and Akkad, though the Sumerians referred to themselves as 'The Black-headed People'."* (28) p-12

There are strong indications that the Sumerian people may have been short and dark. If they are related to the Indus River cultures, this would strengthen this assumption. We do find the small dark complexion traits in people everywhere these traders traveled, Such as the Basque in Spain and the Welsh at the tin mines in Cornwall. We even have a group known as the Scraylings in North America. I must admit, there is no clear evidence that I have found to support this, since the process of inter-marriage quickly fogs the issue.

I do want to say that before they reached Europe they might well be closer in body type to the native people of western India or Tibet. I make this destination, because many would like to assert that these people were what we now call European. I think it is quite clear, as Indo European speaking peoples moved west over Europe, they pushed these traders out. Their philosophy of cooperation and trade were apparently incompatible with constant war. If they were slight in stature compared to the northern invaders, this might have had an influence in their avoidance of war.

G 49 Samitte Armor Pre-Roman Italy, Authors Photo

As can be seen in this photo, the 11-1/2 by 10- 1/4 inch notebook is bigger than the entire breastplate of bronze armor. It is my belief that this is about the size of the original people we are talking about. There is good evidence they might have stopped in Italy.

Religious and Other Characteristics

Story of Gilgamesh: Now I would like to describe some of this culture's key elements during this period. Uruk was once the largest city of Sumer. It was also *"Home of the epic hero, Gilgamesh, now identified as a real king of the city's first dynasty."* (28) p - 64

The epic story of Gilgamesh gives a lot of information about the people of Uruk. It tells us about their relationships with their gods, what they valued, and more. I would like to mention the descriptions of the boats, the description of the journey of Gilgamesh, and the man called Utnapishtim, the *"Farway."*

This story of our hero starts with Gilgamesh meeting Enkidu, a wild man strong enough to be his match. They become friends and are successful in battle. In the meantime, the goddess Ishtar notices Gilgamesh and asks him to be her lover. He refuses and insults her. Then she asks her father, Anu (the sun god), to bring down the "Bull of the Heaven" to smash them.

Anu grants Ishtar's wish and a battle ensues. Our heroes kill the "Bull Of Heaven." This enrages Ishtar even further. Enkidu dreams he will die, and so he does. The gods plan the total destruction of mankind with a flood. One of the gods, Shamash, warns Gilgamesh and tells him to build a boat. Here, we have a very early version of the Noah's Ark story. In another version, Gilgamesh, in his grief over the death of Enkidu, goes on a journey. Some say it is a quest for immortality. He goes with a boatman, Urshanabi the Faraway. He gets to his destination and dives for the magic plant. He gets it, but a serpent steals it. Now, the serpent can change his skin and become young again. Gilgamesh is discouraged, and returns to Uruk and the temple of Ishtar. These stories are in fragments and often cannot be read in their entirety.

In the description of the ark, the builder states he built six decks thereby dividing the boat into seven parts. Some modern writers have wondered if these people had decks on their ships. This story clearly indicates they were well aware of the use of decks to protect the passengers and cargo, and used them as needed. They also talk of shifting the floor planks, which would imply hatches in today's vocabulary. They talk of using asphalt and a measure of oil that was consumed in the caulking.

In the description of his dive for the magic plant, he fastened stones to his feet to carry him deep and used some sort of water pipe, possibly a snorkel to breathe with. This is much like what the Mediterranean divers do today. This tale indicates these peoples were at ease with the sea. It also indicates that they had the technical expertise and material to build large ships or dive for pearls.

It also gives the source of the battle with the sacred bull. In fact, the description of Enkidu grabbing the bull's horns, and Gilgamesh putting his sword between the bull's horns and his neck, brings to mind the Spanish bullfighters of today. Also, the mural in the palace of Knossos, where some sort of ritual performed with the bulls is shown, may have been something like the running of the bulls done today in that area.

I personally believe there is much more to this story than what is found on the surface. After all, this society wrote entire shipping contracts on a two-inch square of clay. I believe this was a story to relate their history. Come with me for a minute, while I make a supposition. Gilgamesh was the priest-king of the city-state Uruk. Enkidu represents the people or culture of some far country like Spain or France. The boatman was a sturdy, experienced captain of a large vessel in the western Mediterranean or the Atlantic. Anu was the Sun and Ishtar was Venus. Because Gilgamesh challenged and berated her by taking his vessel on his great journey, she asked her father, the sun, to make a big storm cell, "The Bull of the Heavens," to smash him. Together, the priest-king, his newfound friends amongst the wild men, and their sturdy boatman beat the storm beast and traveled to the land of Faraway. Then they returned again to the ramparts of Uruk. Although he succeeded in his challenge of Ishtar and completed his trip, he learned wisely that the gods, Anu and Ishtar, would always be out of reach, and mankind's lot was to live and die as a man.

This is a very old story. The actual documents date to about 1500 BC. The actual story must go back to the hay-day of Uruk, 2500 BC, well before 1800 BC when Hammurabi displaced the Sumerian leaders. I am not aware of an actual date the story happened, but 3000 BC seems about right.

Bulls and Cats: Religion of the Sumerian people was similar to that of their Canaanite neighbors. The god, Baal, was sometimes represented as a bull. Presumably a statement of respect, people who were to intercede between God and man often wore horns. Cats were also important in the religious rituals.

G - 50 Bulls and Cats, Author's Sketch Ref. (17) p - 63

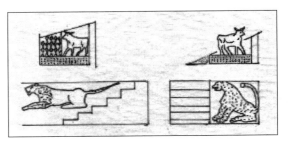

Myths From Mesopotamia: Translator: S. N. Kramer, *The Deluge:* "*After Anu, Enlil, Enki, and Ninhursag had fashioned the black-headed (people). . . .*" The word "black-headed" usually refers to the inhabitants of Sumer and Babylon. In the present context, it seems to refer to mankind as a whole. (20) p - 28

We also find the legend of Gilgamesh written in Hittite and Hurrian, in addition to Old Babylonian (Sumerian) and Assyrian (post Hammurabi Mesopotamian).

The Hittite connection could indicate the legend migrated west onto the Anatolian peninsula's southern shore with the spreading of the priest king phase of the early Sumerian traders. Another source suggests that these people may have originated in the highlands between Turkey, Iraq, and Iran. This is apparently where the copper metal technology first started. One name for them is the Hebernites, the descendants of Heber, the grandson of Noah. The word Hebernite means the oxen, the bull, or the Torrians. This would assume they migrated both east and west from the highland source.

These traders, I believe, were the precursors to the Cypriot/ Minoan cultures. They also would have provided the early trading expertise of the Canaanite and pre-Phoenician cities like Ugarit and Byblos. So far, this can only be assumed since these traders did not totally change the cultures they became part of. The surviving culture was always an amalgam of both cultures. As the Semitic influence increased in the Levant, the Hurrians and Indo-Iranians were absorbed. There is no doubt they provided the trading and sea-going expertise to their new overlords. However, on Crete things were different. The protection the sea afforded, to island kingdoms like Cyprus and Crete, allowed a substantial amount of the cultural beliefs to survive.

By the time the culture in Sumer starts to fade, it has become well established in the Aegean Sea, although somewhat modified by the new circumstances. Here it is given the name Minoan by Evans, and it is at its peak by 1800 BC. I believe it is safe to call the Minoan culture the heirs of the Sumerian culture and trading cousins of both the Semitic led Canaanite culture, and the developing Hittite culture on the Anatolian peninsula.

It is still being led by priest-kings, but by now, the post is inherited. So we can begin to see the start of what may later be called the industrial family cartels. Protection of the seas, along with a moral codex of brotherhood, allows these island kingdoms to get rich on the Copper arms trade of their battling neighbors.

The male god, Anu, has succumbed to the Canaanite version Baal, and the female goddess, Ishtar, although still honored, is no longer supreme but on a par with Baal. The great bull, battled by Gilgamesh, was still honored in the seasonal games for its fertility. In general, the gods were giving way to a pleasant secular lifestyle made possible by the lucrative trade agreements.

The culture was a fun-loving happy people, who worshipped their sun god on mountaintops, painted their walls with pictures of beauty, and quietly plied their skilled trades. They were great seaman with over a thousand years of experience on the seas.

They still feared the great storms, "Bulls of the sky", whipped up by Ishtar, but their priests would study the stars and tell them when it was favorable to sail, and when they should wait. This was probably not born of suspicious fears but of a thousand years of experience. To assume these people were afraid of the sea has no basis. To the contrary, they probably told the stories of monsters to discourage competition.

New Locations New Names

As we travel west, we find more names of the cultures these traders moved through. Marija Gimbutas in her book, *Language of the Goddess*, talks of the Old European Culture. Riane Eisler, in her book, "*The Chalice & The Blade*," supports this idea by pointing out a goddess based religion tied together a group of sites she called the, *Old Europe*. "*The term, Old Europe, was introduced to designate the civilization that lasted from ca. 7000 to 3500 BCE in southeastern Europe, but the term may also be used for all of Europe before the Indo-European invasion, including the megalithic cultures of western Europe (Ireland, Malta, Sardinia, and parts of Great Britain, Scandinavia, France, Spain, and Italy) from the 5th to the 3rd millennium BCE.*" (15) p - 248

This old European culture was in existence, when the Sumerians first started to reach out in their search for raw materials that were needed to fuel the industrial activity of their cities. In fact, many of the skills we attribute to either the Sumerian or the Egyptian cultures may have really been developed in this Neolithic Old European culture—the difference being that smaller villages would not support as much specialization. It is quite possible; the first copper metal work came out of just one such village. It is a matter of record that there is little copper in either Sumer or Egypt, and that copper was used at a very early time in the eastern Turkey highlands.

It is also a matter of record that these cultures had been sailing out to islands and colonizing them, hundreds, if not thousands, of years before the development of cities in Sumer. The boatman in the story of Gilgamesh may well have been a deep-sea whaler or a transporter of Neolithic migrants. Therefore, it can be assumed that the peaceful trade that benefited both parties would move quickly through the established cultures, and, so it did.

We can follow the seaway trade up the west coast of mainland Greece to the island of Corfu. Homer stated:

Corfu was once inhabited by the mythical Phaiakes or Phaeacians. According to Homer, they were a peaceful, prosperous, happy people: un-warlike, mild-mannered and cheerful. They loved to dance, play the kithara and enjoy life. The Phaeacians were the beloved of the Gods. Their first king, Nausithoos, was the son of Poseidon and Periboia, daughter of Eurymedon, king of the Giants. They had originally lived in a place called Hypereia (not yet identified) but were compelled to pack their belongings and depart, because they were constantly being harassed by their neighbors the Cyplopes. Scheria (the ancient name for Corfu), their new home, was an island at the end of the world, where no one could molest them. (29) p - 8,9

This may have been an explanation as to why some of them left Sumer and migrated west into the Aegean. They then made the short hop over to Italy at Tarentum and the Island of Sicily. Then they continued from Sicily and the west coast of Italy on to Sardinia, Malta, southern France, Spain, western France, Great Britain and Ireland. As we can see here, Gimbutas' and Eisler's goddess culture lead us right from the Minoan Island of Crete all the way to Ireland. This will be established in the Tracks in Stone chapter.

To avoid too much duplication, let us look again to see if the Minoan influences are apparent along this route. Yes, we will find it is as indicated later in the book. In this chapter, we are trying to identify and put a name to these people. We can easily see that the Old European culture must have accepted the alliance. But, it is also obvious, that within the large Neolithic populations of Western Europe, the trading Minoan group was for the most part, a minority.

We can find a blending of the religious symbols and activities in Spain. Here is the western most influence of the bull—in a direct fashion. We still have the bullfights today, almost a direct replay of Gilgamesh's victory over the great bull, and the Greek hero's submission and killing of the Minitar. We have the double ax picked up later by the Battle Ax people and the shaft graves, which are found in many of the cultures.

We also find a new name here in Western Europe, The Bell-Beaker or Maritime, Bell-Beaker folks. They used the double ax or battle-ax symbol in this culture on the stones of Stonehenge, which show the deepening relationships of the Megalithic people and the Minoan Marine traders. Now we must make a choice, since I do not plan to add another name to the already confusing list of cultures. Look at our choices:

1. The Sumerians or Black-heads of Sumer
2. Canaanites of the Levant
3. Hittites of Anatolia
4. Kerfiti as named by the Egyptians
5. Sea Peoples as named by the Egyptians
6. Old Europeans
7. Marine Bell-Beaker folks of Western Europe
8. Marine Archaic, of North America
9. Phoenicians as their descendants were named by the Greeks.

The Canaanite name is disqualified, because it better reflects the Semitic of the post Sargon era in Mesopotamia. The Sumerian name was dropped because it is too limited in its scope, even though it was, I believe, the true mother culture of the trade doctrine we are talking about. The Marine Archaic culture of North America was dropped although it was one of our names for the people. It lacks the scope needed to describe a culture. The Keftiu and Sea People names, used by the Egyptians, were dropped, because we do not have cultural descriptions using these names. The Old European culture is too broad, although it describes a basic part of the culture in question.

The two best names seem to be Evan's Minoans, a culture that is being described more each day, and possibly, the Pre-Phoenician or Canaanite culture that is well described in a later period. It is my honest belief these two cultures were one and the same about 2000 BC. However, due to the confusion the Pre-Phoenician name would create, I feel I must stay with the Minoan name. When we incorporate the cultural descriptions of the Minoans that are being developed daily by the archeological community, we do see the source culture of our trading cartel. When we see the end of this culture on Crete, we see the end of our trade cartel. If ever there was a strong cultural center directing these mining operations, it surely came to an end about 1200 BC when the Dorian Greeks overran Crete. There you have it. For these reasons, I will continue to use the name I started with—"Minoan"—to describe this culture and its people.

How Did These Cultures Spread?

There is one last point to be made here. How did these cultures spread? The Greeks make this clear when they describe how the Phoenicians did it a few hundred years later:

> *How did the Phoenicians of the narrow coastal strip of Lebanon and Palestine with their poor resources, political disunity and restricted manpower, manage to settle this network of small communities? The genius of the Carthaginians, like that of the Tyrians in Cyprus, consisted in planting but a small number of colonials and allowing them to mix freely with the local populations. To the Greeks these bastard communities were known as the Libyphoenices of Africa and the Bastulophoenices of Southeastern Spain. (30) p - 118*

In reality, this non-threatening approach was exactly what was necessary to promote trade. The trade and its new technologies would then win over the population, and a new culture would be created.

The description in the tale of Gilgamesh of using the wiles of one of their young women to win over the wild men of a new country is perfect. This is, no doubt, how it often happened in the real world of that time.

It is this exact process that made this trading cartel so hard to follow. Only the most basic religious and cultural beliefs could survive this system. The process of learning and using the local language, however, gives us one of our best and strongest clues. The traders always went back to their simple linear "A & B" syllabary to record the new language. It was just a matter of finding the sounds being used for a word and applying the appropriate symbol. It was, no doubt, the responsibility of these very first early emissaries to bridge the language barrier. Only this process can explain the use of the exact same syllabary to write both the ancient Basque language and the Cree language. It also may explain the creation of the numerous Ogham codes of Ireland and possibly the Runes of the Baltic. More will be said on this in the chapter about language.

Our Minoan trade cartel moved out across the world, using emissaries where populations existed, and settlers where they did not. This whole process seems unnecessary to agricultural based societies. But to island based societies, trade is the only economic activity that creates wealth. Trade, because trade is the way of life, explains the only reality left for people who have been driven from the rich land of their forefathers by war. Life from the sea, and on the sea, was all they had left. In time, instead of a negative fate, this belief system became the by-word of this culture.

These people would make the ideal trading partners to the Old Copper Culture and the Algonquin. They would move in with and marry into the families of their host and then orchestrate the mining and shipping of copper.

7 Tracks in Stone

Can we show the connection? I think the answer is yes. Remember we do not need to show that some specific Minoan king was in North America trading 4500 years ago. All we need to show is that some process existed for Middle Eastern or European technology to be involved, and that in this process, the mining and removal of the copper from Lake Superior and from North America took place.

This chapter will establish the links to show these connections. One key point was the Sun-god religion. The bull was recognized as a sign of virility and power in this structure. It is evident one other association took a strong hold at this time. The Father-sun impregnating Mother-earth brought the beginning of the end to the Goddess religion in the fully agricultural areas. It also ushered in the sun god as the primary god of the universe in most places.

This relationship was nowhere more important than in the north, where seasons were short and Father-sun was often absent, or nearly so. In England and Ireland, it was the study and honoring of this relationship that led to two of the largest sun altars in the world—Stonehenge in southern England and New Grange in Northern Ireland. Both of these ceremonial sites made it possible to honor the important days when Father-sun started back to impregnate Mother-earth. Celebrations took place on the spring equinox or in some groups, May Day. The long tunnel (as in New Grange) where the Father's bright rays traveled deep into the earth mother to trigger the new growth of spring, have long been recognized as calendar sites. However, I believe they were much more to these early people.

This critical religious and secular information was so important in the everyday lives of the people; it could not be left to memory alone. The exact days of winter solstice, the equinox, summer solstice, and fall equinox were very important. These annual cycles or rhythms gave meaning and balance to the daily work of these cultures. This was the reason for the use of circles—first Woodhenge, then Stonehenge. What better display of Father-sun's faithful returning cycle, and his re-appearance each year exactly as predicted by the religious leaders.

Like their sun altars, the monolith users came to depend on large stones to mark other important places, such as, the burial places of important leaders. Even when they moved into the more specialized professions like traders, or metal workers, their Sun-God symbols were taken along. They set them up at their seasonal outposts. Eventually, we have equinox marks and calendar sites (stone circles) far from the farm based Neolithic centers. It is obvious they are no longer used only as important secular calendars, but they are now a part of the religious and spiritual ceremonies.

It is for this reason, I believe, that we find calendar sites, dolmen, and standing stones in the rocky Laurentian Shield country of Ontario, Canada, and in some of the northern lake states like Minnesota and Michigan. This country was not used for farming. The only real remaining reason for this culture being here was for the mining of copper, lead, silver, and gold.

It is no surprise then to find these monolithic stones scattered among the ancient mine sites. The activity went on for a thousand years. The stones would come to represent recognition and security to these miners thousands of miles from home. No wonder they started to erect large standing stones, to guide their crews into safe harbors, or special portages over various divides. No wonder they carved their names on them, or the name of their god, "Baal." They were intended to honor.

These very normal religious activities that we call *"rituals"* today, gives us clues to track the movements of our sun worshipping traders.

The Tracks

In his book, *The World of Megaliths*, Jean-Pierre Mohan does a beautiful job locating and dating the various megalithic structures. He points out their obvious connections to travel by sea. The use of islands as temple sites, or other special sites is hard to miss. The fact that the sites originated early, before the spread of copper metal usage, is not critical to this work. It just supports what we have already stated; the structures grew out of the beliefs and activities of the existing Neolithic cultures. These cultures were already trading in other items before the copper came into the picture.

Now, over three thousand years have passed and these stones still stand as footprints across the world. They are footprints of a culture that was awakened at the beginning of Neolithic Age, a people who honored the bull and the sun. The two points of the bull's horns may have come to mean consecration of the male and female, the duality of the creative process, the twins of their creation myths, and even possibly, the morning and evening stars of Venus. This was not a part of all cultures, but it was part of a very special trading culture that spread from the eastern Mediterranean outward in both directions—east by sea to India and beyond, and west by sea all the way to Lake Superior and beyond.

We can see evidence that it started in the early Neolithic farmers of Catal Huyuk and Crete. It was carried west by ship to Malta, Sardinia, southern France, Minorca, and finally mainland Spain. Then it proceeded through the Straits of Gibraltar to Portugal, western France (Brittany), southern England, and Ireland. Then perhaps, by purpose or by chance, they went across to New England, Hudson Bay, or down the St. Lawrence and Ottawa Rivers to Sault Ste. Marie, Michigan across the great lake, "Kitchi-Gummi," and into northern Minnesota. I believe these ideas of sun worship and the use of great stones were carried on the ships of early copper miners between 2400 BC and 1200 BC.

The Monolithic stones along this tract do make it evident that these early Neolithic cultures had a strong fishing and sea trade element among them at a very early period. It was already well established by 3000 BC. Also, it is evident that this trade or religious network connected a group of islands and peninsula points all the way from Crete to Ireland and beyond to the Orkneys of northern Scotland.

The Procession went like this:

> Cyprus, Crete, Corfu,
> West of the Greek mainland, "The Heal" of the Italian Boot.
> Sicily, Malta, Sardinia (Italian)
> Corsica (French)
> Minorca and Majorca (off the coast of Barcelona Spain)
> Almeria (on the Spanish mainland)
> Lisbon (a Portugal Atlantic port)
> Oviedo Province (north coast of Spain on the Atlantic)
> Brittany Province (in western France on the Atlantic)
> Salisbury plain, Stonehenge, Isle of Wight (south England)
> Belfast, New Grange Complex (northern Ireland)
> Hebrides Islands (off the Scotland coast)
> Orkney Islands (north of Scotland)

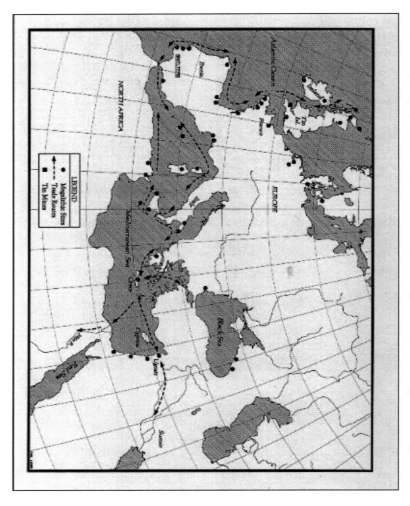

G - 51 Map of European Megaliths, Ref. (33) p - 67

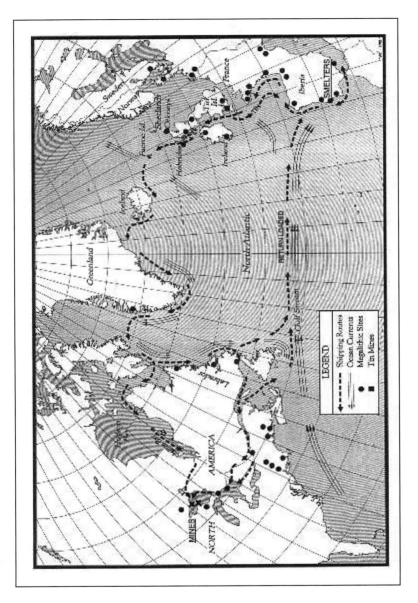

G - 52 Map of North American Megaliths

One thing that is very obvious is that each of these locations has an excellent well-protected port. Many of these port settlements are on islands, which also afforded a natural built-in protection. They usually seem to be a few hundred miles apart. This could lead a person to believe they may have been strategically placed to support a shipping trade route. This cannot be verified since inland sites can also be found. However, the inland cultures do vary some from the maritime sites.

The fact that these European megalithic sites existed has never been questioned. However, there has been substantial controversy about who built them, and why. We will shed very little light on that issue in this book. All we want to do is point out that these megalithic structures, especially the long boroughs, standing stones, stone circles, and dolmen appear to be located along this particular sea route from Crete to the Tin Isles. This was, in all probability, the same route taken by the early metal workers in search of raw materials.

Near the end of the monolithic period about 1200 BC, they seem to represent two different aspects of the same culture. The metal workers and the builders of the long boroughs appear to be the same people. Some would even call them the Maritime Bell-Beaker Culture.

To my knowledge, no one has ever searched for standing stones or dolmen sites farther west then Ireland, such as, on Denmark's Faeroe Islands, or on the shores of Iceland. This could be very interesting especially if some are found. We do know they show up again on Greenland and the North American continent. They are in the Canadian Maritimes, New England, and west through Ontario to Lake Superior and into Minnesota. This has not been broadly reported since, in my opinion, our archeological community cannot readily explain it.

The New England Antiquities Research Association (NEARA) says there are over a hundred sites in New England and New York. (51)

Our small northern Michigan group associated with ISAC, the Institute for the Study of American Cultures, has documented five sites in Michigan and Minnesota. The Canadians also have some sites in Ontario and the Maritimes.

Taken as a whole, these standing stones and monolithic structures clearly mark a trail, possibly that of the early metal traders. It should also be pointed out that copper was not the only mineral that this group was known to mine. There is evidence they were also taking gold, silver and lead, but this is another topic we will not explore here. Our intent is to stay focused on the early mining of Lake Superior copper.

The religious belief systems of this culture were no longer relevant in Europe, after the Romans invaded and conquered the literate world about 150 BC. They crushed the monuments and laughed at the superstitions.

The Roman governors were far removed from the spiritual side of life. They had secular laws to govern the people and calendars to tell when to plant crops.

Only in the secret societies of the Celtic Druid monks did any knowledge of the stones persist. Even this was scattered and condemned as devil worship by the Christian teachers the Romans brought along. Most of the monuments were physically destroyed, because they were said to be the works of the devil. What was not destroyed was driven underground during the Inquisitions and witch burnings. Thousands who believed in the simple spirituality of the natural world were killed. The stones could talk no more to those with no ears to hear. This is still a problem to many.

I saw this with sadness at first, but now the mere fact that I can write this without being burned at the stake is something. I am not asking you to think as I do, but I am suggesting you cannot keep these stones silent forever. People are starting to hear these ancient messages from the past. These are people who are no longer threatened by the denials of the establishment. These stones are footprints, footprints from the copper mines of Lake Superior to the smelters of the Iberian Peninsula and on to the warehouses in Ugarit or the Levant. They represent a route that lead from the mines on Lake Superior to the Bronze Age cultures of Egypt and Mesopotamia, and their armies of conquest outfitted and shielded by copper and bronze.

Some may ask the question, "Do these stones really have any connection to the copper trade or the Minoan culture for that matter?" To strengthen the connection for you, the reader, I want to examine the early history of five locations along the route: Spain, France, England, Ireland and New England area of the USA.

Along the Monolithic Track

Iberian Peninsula, Tarshish (Cadiz) and (Lisbon): Back in our early Christian Bible, we hear of the ships of Tarshish. Some people think this is in reference to a group of traders in Spain, possibly located at Cadiz, or the massive ancient Reo Tinto Mine. However, we need not make suppositions; it is a well-accepted fact that the Phoenician culture of about 800 BC traded this far west.

It is not so clearly accepted, but according to Grolier Electronic Encyclopedia, 1992, there is some support for the idea that a monolithic trade group, we may even call them Pre-Phoenicians, did stop there much earlier. Let me quote them here:

The Beaker culture is a name given to a group of communities responsible for the spread of copper metallurgy in Europe in the third millennium BC. . . . The second major Beaker tradition probably originated in Iberia, (Spain & Portugal). The vessels of the southern Beaker people are distinguished by their bell-shaped profile. The Bell-Beaker or Maritime-Beaker culture, as it is sometimes called, developed out of the local culture represented at Villa Nova de Sao Pedro in Portugal, from which the Beaker people adopted copper metallurgy. Radio carbon dating suggests that this happened around 2500 BC. From Iberia, Bell-Beaker culture spread to France, Britain, and ultimately to Germany and the low-countries. A fusion of traditions resulted in northwest Europe, Beaker people being influenced by the battle-ax culture. . . . In Britain, the beaker people are associated with some major ritual monuments, including Avebery in Woltshire. (25) Beaker culture.

Although the monolithic tie here is not strongly defined, we know there are monolithic stone structures on the Iberian Peninsula and its islands—one of these is mentioned by Hawkins. *"The Taulas of Minorca, eighteen megalithic monuments were orientated to the sun and moon." (32) p - 121*

The mountains and the sea gave substantial isolation and protection to the river estuaries and valleys where they met the sea. These rich soils and good harbors were the ideal locations for the Maritime Beaker villages. Harrison describes this below:

It is on the Lisbon and Setubal peninsulas of central Portugal, where the rivers Tagus and Sado widen out into estuaries, that nearly all of the Portuguese Beaker sites are located. Over one hundred of all kinds have been found . . . Favored as much by climate as by its' geography, this region supported one of the richest and most populous Copper Age societies of the third millennium in Iberia, and it is upon the settlements and in the tombs of these people that early Maritime beakers are nearly always found. (31) p - 128

It is characterized by fortified settlements, small hamlets and a wide variety of megalithic tombs and small caves for collective burial. The earliest periods of this culture are obscure, but by 2400-2300 BC it had a flourishing copper industry making axes, chisels, knives and awls in quantity, and a great variety of luxury objects. . . . (31) p - 128

France, Brittany: The western province of Brittany has the most monolithic evidence in France. Of primary importance are the sites related to the Maritime group. These are the most likely representatives of the culture we are interested in. Mohen has mapped out fourteen of these sites in his book. Some of these sites are very advanced. I was unable to visit and photograph sites in France but that does not mean they do not exist. (33) p-155

England, Stonehenge: In more recent times, the enigma of the stones (like Stonehenge) has melted away under the increase in technological advances. Carbon dating, for example, now tells us a time frame for Stonehenge, the greatest of these monuments. It also gives us a name for the people who were there to make and use it.

Richard Harrison in his book, *The Beaker Folk, Copper Age Archaeology in Western Europe*, does an excellent job putting together the chronology and movement of the "Beaker Folk." He places the Beaker Folk there during the construction of the Henge.

Jean-Pierre Mohen does a good job laying out the chronological stages of Stonehenge:

> *Stonehenge l,*   *3100-2300 BC.*
> *Stonehenge ll,*   *2300-2100 BC.*
> *Stonehenge llla*   *2100-2000 BC.*
> *Stonehenge lllb*   *2000-1500 BC.*
> *Stonehenge lllc*   *1500-1100 BC.* (33) p -130

G 53 Stonehenge, Author's Photo

Mr. Mohen recognizes Beaker objects at Stonehenge, but he does not seem ready to admit they built it. In contrast, Mr. Harrison states:

> *Beaker pottery is also intimately associated with many of the great ritual monuments in the British Isles. . . . Much the same can be said of the great Wessex Ceremonial centers at Avebury and Stonehenge where major excavation has shown that the Beaker communities played an important roll in both the construction and remodeling. This activity was matched at Stonehenge where Beaker shreds are known to be stratified in the silting from the ditches as well as from various parts of the interior. They are generally associated with phase two of the monument's, radiocarbon dated around 1700-1600, when the circle of blue stones was set up on a new alignment towards the midsummer sunrise.* (31) p - 94, 95

These two authors may quibble some about the dates of the "Bell Beaker" associations, but they both concur that these people were there around 2000 BC to 1600 BC. The question that still seems unresolved is, "Were they there at the very first construction?" My assumption is, the Bell-Beaker pots may not have been present, but the Beaker people probably were. Remember, we believe the reason for these large ceremonial centers was to mark and honor the relationship between Father Sun and Mother Earth of these sun-worshipping societies.

More importantly, what we must not overlook is that the Beaker people were the first copper and bronze using people in the area. The colonized settlements were in close association with local sources of copper and tin. A second major point is that they were definitely a water based, sea-going folk. In fact, some archaeologist have pointed out that the early Beakers were not associated with the villages. The unusual distribution of the pottery leads some researchers to believe this item may be related to trade. I believe this is the logical assump-tion to make.

When speaking about the fact that most Beaker findings come from graves, Harrison states, *"The result is that we are well informed about the dead and a few select aspects of their society, but we know next to nothing about the economic base of their lives."* (31) p - 14

Without going into too much detail here, the concept of colonial villages established to support a far reaching trade network to secure copper could well explain the unusual distribution of these vessels and their association with the first copper and bronze artifacts.

There is a final story, if you will, about the Beaker Folk. They introduced into the formerly un-stratified (without a hierarchy) Neolithic society, "*the concentration of private wealth in the hands of a few people, the rise of Chieftains and their consorts.*" (31) p-8

This same storyline we find everywhere—merchant sovereigns colonize. The emphasis is then put on religious ceremonies to tie the people together; the merchant kings then utilize this power-base to secure a stable trading partner. Although the trade benefits everyone and keeps the system going, the merchant king always becomes the richest. This religious organization also made it possible to organize the large numbers of people to complete Herculean tasks like building Stonehenge or New Grange. This would also allow them to mine 50 million pounds of copper—two months travel to the west of their home base.

We also have another author, Gerald Hawkins, an astronomer, whose book is entitled, *Stonehenge Decoded;* it gives us a similar view of Stonehenge:

> *Beginning about 1700 B.C. the Bronze Age proper came to Britain, and with it the final wave of construction at Stonehenge. This date is fixed within a hundred years or so by radiocarbon dating of a deer antler found buried in the fill around stone 56. (32) p - 50*
>
> *The building of Stonehenge I, which began about 1900 B.C., lasted for an indeterminate number of years. Perhaps several decades several decades were required for the various diggings and stone and wood column preparation and placement. . . . We cannot know what these earliest builders were like, nor what they felt and thought about their first handiwork, . . ." (32) p - 47*
>
> *About 1750 B.C. the second wave of construction at Stonehenge began. This work was done, apparently, by a different race of people: the Beaker people.*
>
> *These second builders brought the first assembly of megaliths, or "large stone." At least 82 blue stones, weighing up to five tons each, were to be set up in two concentric circles around the center of the enclosure, about 6 feet apart and 35 feet from the center. . . . This bank-bordered roadway, now almost obliterated, originally went northeast from the Stonehenge entrance and curved right to the river Avon, some two miles away. The avenue was probably used as a road for hauling blue stone from the river to the monument. (32) p - 48.*

It was obvious that it was taken off some sort of boat or ship. They probably would have traveled a total water distance of 215 miles.

The last builders were, apparently, the powerful, rich, commercially active Wessex people. They were excellent craftsmen who possessed quite sophisticated tools and ornaments and weapons, of gold as well as bronze. They seem to have organized themselves into groups led by warrior chieftains, but they probably preferred trading to fighting. There is strong evidence that they were in communication with the great contemporary Mediterranean civilizations of Minoan Crete, Mycenaean Greece, Egypt, and the ancestors of the traveling-trading Phoenicians. (32) p - 50,51

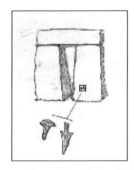

G 54 Carving on StonehengeAuthor's Sketch (39) p - 74

Atkinson inclines seriously to this theory, stressing the importance of the evidence of a dagger carving and ax carvings as well as Mediterranean artifacts found in the burial of Stonehenge, and pointing out that Stonehenge is unique not only in the elegance of its construction but also in the fact that it is the only stone monument known to have been built by Wessex people. Therefore, it would seem not to have been part of a local building tradition, another in a continuing series, but a rara avis—a Minerva sprung full-grown from some father's brow without ever having a childhood. Now how could such a complex structure, embodying very subtle, advanced concepts and even more advanced building techniques, have risen from nothing? (32) p 48 - 51

Now we know that they quarried and moved by ship the 82 huge blue stones, which make up the circle at the Henge—a feat similar to the well known transporting of the construction blocks for the Egyptian pyramids. Here, also, we have an actual connection to the Minoan culture. It is obvious that the necessary shipping technology to move the copper ore had reached the British Isles by this time (approximately 2100 BC).

Just to verify why the Bronze Age copper miners were in England this early, I would like to quote a short passage from J. A. Buckley's book, *The Cornish Mining Industry.*

"Artifacts found on the tin sites, and identified by archeologists, indicate that the tin industry was established by the Early Bronze Age (2100-1500 BC), and was widespread by the Middle Bronze Age" (1500-800 BC).

"Historical references support this. They show a well established and fairly sophisticated tin trade between Cornwall and the Mediterranean by the 4th century BC." (36) p - 3

The reader should be aware that this does not mean this is when the trade started, only when it showed up in the historical record. More recently, work by a small number of dedicated individuals has located about 30 ancient copper mining sites in England.

All of the sites were in use during the Bronze Age. Ross Island appears to be the earliest, with dates clustering in the second half of the 3rd millennium BC (2500 to 2000 BC). This is just prior to the beginning of the early Bronze Age in Ireland—the period associated with the introduction of metallurgy in the British Isles. The other sites were all in use at much the same time spanning the early Bronze Age and earlier Middle Bronze Age from c 1900–1200BC. But what of the evidence for the copper they produced?" (48) p - 4

This last quote make it clear someone was expanding the copper mining business west into England and Ireland around 2500 BC. This is earlier than is generally recognized, but it fits exactly into our carbon date at the mines on Lake Superior (2470 BC). It also coincides with the end of the trade, 1200 BC.

This work asks one other question of significance. Where does the nickel come from? Apparently some English bronze has nickel content. Maybe they should look at the copper mines of Ontario where much nickel is now being produced.

Ireland: Here is another excellent example to describe the trail left by the megalithic copper traders. Because of its out-of-the-way location, the Mesolithic culture (Pre-Neolithic Agriculture) still existed with, *"little change over a period of almost 3000 years, suggesting that the people there continued to live in comparative isolation in the same area over a number of millennia"* . . . *"c. 6240 - c.3465 bc."* (34) p - 25

The arrival of the farmers in the fourth millennia was clearly and dramatically shown in the abrupt changes of lifestyle. This change had spread to Europe from Mesopotamia over two routes, *"one by land along the Danube into central and northwestern Europe and the other by sea across the Mediterranean to Spain and France, as far as the straits of Dover."* (34) p - 27

It is this sea expansion we are interested in pinpointing better. A plank house, constructed in 3215 BC, gives us the best usable date. This fits well into the pollen dates for the spread of farming between 3895 BC and 2965 BC. These Neolithic farmers (Beaker folk) proceeded to build, ". . . *the great passage tomb at New Grange which provided a radiocarbon date of c. 2500 BC but which is likely to have been built 600 years earlier around 3100 BC. "* (34) p-10

This religious structure of these people did not originate in Ireland. The Beaker people brought it in when they colonized the place. They also brought in sheep, goats, and cattle, which were not found in Ireland before they arrived. It is believed they were imported around 3430 BC. This tells us a lot about how the colonizing took place. The colonist and their cattle and sheep were loaded on big ships and transported to the suitable locations. No doubt, promises of land and trade went along with the process. The religious centers were quickly built. This allowed the merchant or sun-worshipping priest-kings a measure of organization and control. Sites, such as this great site at New Grange, dot the countryside. There are also numerous Henge and Stone circle sites in the same part of Ireland. These date to around 2000 BC.

G - 55 New Grange Interior Author's Sketch (33) p - 269

Were these colonists really *"Beaker Folk"*? I think the answer to this is yes. *"Different from Britain here the beaker pottery is associated with domestic activity, as we have seen at New Grange, Knowth, Ballynagilly, Dalkey Island, and Lough Gur."* (34) p - 90

It is evident to me there were few, if any, Neolithic farmers here when the Beaker traders arrived. They took this opportunity to set up their own kick-off point for the trips west. The New Grange site is one of the most sophisticated sun sites in existence.

This connection between Beakers and megalithic is, however, also something which Ireland shares in common with Brittany and other areas of the Atlantic Europe, where Bell Beakers, popular in Ireland, also are found. (34) p - 91

This predilection for the northern half of Ireland in the distribution of Beaker pottery can also be followed in items such as the tanged copper dagger, archer's wrist guards and the v-perforated buttons, which are usually associated with Beaker pottery in Britain and on the Continent, though never found together with it in Ireland. (34) p - 91

A substantial number of flat copper ax molds were also found. A dagger and ax mold was both found on the same rock. Also, a bronze ax was found at New Grange with an approximate date of 2100 to 1935 BC. An interesting thing happened in Ireland around 1200 BC:

The vigorous industry which began to flourish in the period around 1200 BC, and which is most easily exemplified in the Bishopsland hoard, is one which was not anticipated in the immediately proceeding centuries. It introduces a freshness into a long-established traditional industry. (34) p -131

The "action-reaction" stimulus here could be expected. Ireland's New Grange Community, primarily one of purely "Beaker Folk" (a possible Minoan Settlement), was the ideal respite for some of the skilled craftsmen from Crete. No doubt, as the take-over by the Dorian Greeks became evident on their homeland, some of the craftsmen took their families and slipped on the next ship out to Ireland, where they may even have had kin. Enough of this took place for it to show up in the archaeological record. This is, of course, only part of my hypothesis showing up a little early.

In their westward expansion, our Minoan traders have acquired a new name, "The Beaker Folk." Perhaps, I should say, by blending with the locals they have created a new culture called the "Beaker Folk or the Maritime Beaker Culture."

We should not get too hung up on this beaker pottery, it could be something as simple as a milk or beer bottle. Neither of these items may have been used much back in the sheep and wine cultures of Crete. However, they found a real niche in northern Europe.

Do the beakers come west to North America? I am not sure. Maybe what this pot was used for was not used at the mine sites. As an example, there would be no need for a milk bottle on Lake Superior. Remember, in Europe they did not show up at a lot of the village sites. Their use was quite specific. However, the stone monuments and sun worship calendar sites did make the trip. Also, the designs of a lot of the copper artifacts are identical to those found on our side of the Atlantic.

Iceland & Greenland: Iceland can well be thought of as the stepping-stone to the new world. A quirk of fate, on how maps and charts are generally made (basically flat), has introduced into the thinking of most Americans that from North America to Ireland or Norway is a long way across the continents. This is understandable, since most maps show Iceland and Greenland much expanded, just to fill in the space on the map. Nothing could be further from the truth. You can literally walk the few miles across the ice on the north end of Baffin Bay to Greenland. From the mountains of Greenland's east coast, you can see the mountains of Iceland across the Denmark Strait—a mere 180 miles. Some geographers actually consider Iceland part of North America.

From Norway to Iceland it was considered a six or seven day sail, with the Faeroes Islands about halfway there. In good weather, you may only be out of sight of land one or two days. Some sailors say, on occasion, you can see mountain tips on both land masses from the middle. It is just a little over five hundred miles to Scotland from the east shore of Iceland.

This is not to imply the crossing was not dangerous to these little single mast sailing ships. Knowing all this, it seems quite plausible, that sailors from the Orkneys or the Hebrides could easily have made the trip. The original driving force may have been new fishing grounds, or for whale hunting, or ivory hunting of walrus tusks. We know these were all valuable commodities to the early inhabitants of these waters.

The Norse record, of a six to seven-day trip from Norway to Iceland, implies travel of about 3.5 miles per hour. This is a good speed for these ships and was probably done with favorable winds. There would be no reason to assume our traders could not do equally as well. If they actually went to the Faeroes Islands, they would probably only be out of sight of land for one day on average, and the trips would only be three days long. You could then hold up at the Faeroes and wait for another weather pattern, then make the next leg of the journey.

Now the question arises. Was there ever any evidence that this might actually have happened? We know that when the current settlers of Iceland, the Norwegians, arrived in approximately 795 AD, there were already Irish monks inhabiting this region. This would be the right people if our assumptions are correct, but the period is much too late. We have no clue as to how long these monks were there at this time. This is weak evidence, but helpful.

A stronger statement comes from the Greek Pytheas explorations of 325 BC. He records a place called the "Ultima Thule" North of Scotland.

Some say this is in Norway. However, Columbus referred to Iceland as "Thula" when he traveled there in 1477 AD. Stefansson says it this way:

> *We are now predisposed to think not merely that Pytheas visited Iceland around 325 BC. But also that implications of his statement it is correct—that he was informed about Iceland before he visited it, by the people of the British Isles, who may have been familiar with it a few more or even many centuries before. (37) p - xv*

To carry this back to our very early period, we look once more at Stefansson's book. Here he is talking about why some archeologists are changing views on the subject:

> *A statement of the new Archeologist position was made by A.W. Brogger, director of the National Museum of Norway in his Presidential address to an International Congress of Archaeologist at Oslo in 1936. There he treated as an established fact the Idea of a Golden Age of Navigation which was at its height surely 1500 years before Christ, and that it may have been on a high level for as much as a thousand years or even two thousand years before. During this golden age, man is pictured as having swarmed over the Atlantic, discovering all the islands and plying between the continents that lie east and west of the ocean. (37) p - xv*

Here we have a man who was responsible for the archeological treasures of Norway, saying that Iceland and all these islands were probably explored and settled two thousand years before the birth of Christ. I do not know what evidence he had to make such a statement, but, no doubt, he had considerable evidence available to him. Thanks to carbon dating, we now know of a culture known as the Sag gag Culture who were on Greenland about 1500 BC. There may be similar information available about Iceland and some of the other islands. Some say the first Inuit people—Skraelings to the Norsemen—first appeared about four to five thousand years ago. They were found on the north east of Hudson Bay. They were a small people, at least, to the Norsemen.

One of the researchers studying in this field told me that the Inuit speak of a three-toed god on their island of Greenland. We are assuming this is a large dolmen. I have no documented proof of this. Another interesting story came to me through a friend. Although they were reluctant to say exactly what they found, two young Canadian writers,

Gary and Joanie McGuffin, who wrote *Where Rivers Run,* found old stone works that may date to a very early period on the south west end of Greenland. I have not seen any actual documentation on either subject. The Inuit have adapted and use the Cree syllabary even to this day, probably because it fits their language so much better than the Latin alphabet.

This quick search of the records indicates support for our theory, that our Minoan or some other traders did island hopping across the North Atlantic 3500-plus years ago. The information, though sketchy, has not been well publicized. This is the treatment information receives, if it does not support the system's view. I would like to pursue the study of the North Atlantic more, but neither time nor money allows it.

New England: There is an interesting story published in the New England Antiquities Research Association Journal, Volume # XXVIII. No 1 and 2, dated Summer and Fall 1993. The article was entitled, *"The Marriage of Earth and Sky"* by C J Hancock. Mr. Hancock goes on to express with a brief five photographs and two paragraphs how the ancients constructed a cave or light chamber into which a shaft of light from the winter solstice sun penetrates the chamber to the exact end. As it leaves, its last rays light up a vulviform carving on one of the foundation. *"A phallic stone, found near by and inscribed . . . to inseminate the Goddess . . . states a theme reiterated in various ways at the Calendar II Site."* (35) p - 10

I believe the striking resemblance of this story to the New Grange site in Ireland tells the real story of the New Grange, the marriage of Earth (Mother) and Sky (Father). It reveals New Grange as possibly being a large spring ceremonial site. The only difference is this ceremonial site, being described by C.J. Hancock, is here in Vermont, USA. This site, and many like it, are scattered about in what I have called the traders over-winter area in southern New England.

American Stonehenge: A second site, known as the American Stonehenge, also begs the comparison. This site has numerous solar and astronomical alignments, but it has one more extremely sun worshipper artifact, a sacrifice table. To my knowledge, it is the only one found in the northeastern United States of America.

This site is well researched, privately, but is not taken seriously by the New England Archeologist profession. It has been carbon dated to the period of 1995 BC. The site has numerous stone structures, most poorly understood. It is well worth the trip to see it.

G - 56 Sacrifice Table, Author's Photo

Stone Chambers: I was able to visit numerous stone chambers of which I photographed two excellent examples. The first had an opening as high as my head, six plus feet. It was thirty-four feet deep. The capstones spanned a four and one half foot corbel arch. This one was perfectly aligned to the winter solstice sunrise.

G - 57 Winter Solstice Stone Chamber, Author's Photo

A second chamber only two hundred feet from the first is slightly smaller. The compass indications are that this one is aligned to the equinox sunrise. The colonists did not maintain the second site so it is not in as good of state of repair. It is my personal opinion that these sites could be thousands of years old and that they were maintained by the Algonquin culture up until the white man came.

G - 58 Equinox Stone Chamber, Author's Photo

The fact that these sites used corbel construction with large quarried stone slabs should not be ignored. These slabs were often about two feet wide and six to eight feet long. The Minoans commonly used corbel construction technique. While the colonists were surely aware of the process, there is little evidence they used it much. One New England stonemason is to have said, *"Why would they do it? It is very difficult. They would just use wood for a roof."*

New York Dolmen: I was also able to visit and photograph a large dolmen. It was the biggest I have seen. It was about ten feet high and forty-five feet around. It had been carefully erected on three groups of stones. One stone slipped but the other two groups had been carefully shimmed to keep them together. I have included a photo of this dolmen and one photo of the shimmed base supports. This fine artifact is being protected by the local population, but it was for years misidentified as a glacial erratic. Apparently no one has the courage to officially call it what it really was until just recently. The sign has been modified to read, *"Some think it is a dolmen"*.

G 59 Salem New York Dolmen, Author's Photo

G 60 Shimmed Support of Dolmen

New England has extensive mega-lithic monuments. NEARA and their associates have mapped hundreds. A large number have also been found in the Hudson River Valley. This culture is the largest group of monolithic people in North America. There is no accepted archeological tradition that explains their existence. This will soon be remedied, I am sure. The New England folks are quietly gathering information that the intellectual community will not be able to continue to ignore.

I believe there is a very strong possibility that this culture provided the over-winter location for the first wave of Lake Superior miners, a culture some are starting to call the "Maritime Archaic" or "Red Paint People." Both the names and the description fit our Minoan traders in their new association with the Pre-Algonquian group. The Pre-Algonquian group will be discussed further in the section on language.

New England's Archeological Record: As I was putting together the last chapter of this book, it became evident that if the Wisconsin and Irish archeological records had clues that tied down this theory and the significant dates, then surely New England should also have some important evidence. Of course, I had the stone monuments and sites and the Algonquian language. However, one of my friends advised me to use actual archeological data whenever possible. This he reasoned would be better accepted by the profession at large. Of course, he is right and in reality, the archeologists are the only ones who keep the accurate records necessary to verify the theory.

I reasoned that if even a small number of Minoan traders moved in with the Algonquian people in New England, their agricultural technology would surely be changed, and this would show up in the archeological record. The book that I was able to find on the subject is called, *Emergent Horticultural Economies of The Eastern Woodlands* by William F Keegan. It is an assemblage of papers on the subject from a conference of the same name.

It seems that people, trying to track the development of agriculture in the northeastern United States, are having difficulty making sense out of it. Apparently, some corn has been dated in the North Beach Phase of Early Woodland in the Long Island area at approximately 700 BC to 500 BC. This is about the same time it shows up in the southwestern United States, but no real Maize Culture really develops till much later. The Maize Culture did not show up in the northeast until only a few hundred years before Columbus.

Although this paper by Thomas J. Rily was interesting, it appeared the corn stirring the controversy came from southern Florida, it was not the evidence I needed. Rily did go on to imply, that the connection between agriculture and the woodland culture is not what is expected in New England.

A second article by Kevin A. McBride and Robert E. Dewar of the University of Connecticut (ref. 38) provided exactly the type of evidence I expected to find.

The following information points out several recognizable changes that take place just when and where you would expect them to, if my hypothesis were correct. The first and probably the most important was the technological advance that took place during the end of the archaic period (2213 BC to 1313 BC in the Lower Connecticut River valley). In the Tinkham Phase or the Narrow-Stemmed Tradition, the long-term storage of a native seed called Chenopodium (a plant of the Goose-foot family) was a key part of this local aboriginal economy. This information is reinforced by the discovery of the carbonized exoskeleton of a granary weevil (Sitophilus Granarius). This was from a feature that also had the Chenopodium seeds. This was firmly dated at a site known as the "Woodchuck Site" from 1713 BC to 1213 BC. I was elated with this discovery, because here again, the record supported the theory. Here, we have evidence of an entire archeological phase at exactly the right time with a newly introduced technology—long-term seed storage of a local food seed. This was not an introduced grain as some might expect but a significant up-grade of a locally used food source. The only thing introduced was probably a simple storage container and the idea that if a lot of grain was gathered and kept dry, it would allow for other activities such as mining as well as providing winter security.

The settlement pattern also reflected change. A large number of seasonal foraging camps were established, presumably to augment a new technology. This activity began about 2213 BC with the advent of the new Tinkham phase of the culture, and ended in 1213 BC, when everything seemed to change back. Is this Tinkham phase really just the existing culture after contact with our traders?

The Salmon River archeological phase, 1313 BC to 713 BC, seemed to reflect a reduction in the extensive foraging and a return to living on the riverbanks. This could well reflect the end of our mining period. One date is 1313 BC, and the other is 1213 BC. This matches amazingly well to the 1200 BC date we have assigned as the end of the first phase of mining. It also matches the end of the use of the large copper tools by the Wisconsin Copper Complex group. It would be interesting to know if the Tinkham phase started using copper needles and fishhooks. It seems logical they would; there may also be changes in the boat and fishing technologies that could also be dated.

Regardless of these unanswered questions, one question was definitely answered. The archeological record of the lower Connecticut River valley provided strong evidence of a possible Minoan miner contact. The new storage technology, and even the granary pest that may have been introduced, are there in the record.

The changes in the settlement pattern that are not yet explained to anyone's satisfaction are best stated by a quote from Kevin A. McBride and Robert E. Dewar in their article:

> *We conclude that the interpretation of the woodland prehistory in Connecticut has been twisted by the false assumption that sedentism, ceramic production, and population aggregation are "consequences" of the adoption of agriculture. The explanation of woodland settlement patterns and ecology in the Connecticut River Valley has yet to be written.* (38) p - 324

It is my belief that when the copper trade connection is introduced into the New England equation, the answers will just pour out—the unusual foraging patterns, the task specific camps, the temporary nature of so many camps, and finally its abrupt end in 1200 BC, only to be picked up again during the second phase of the trade and mining in about 700 BC. The archeologists of New England know something is wrong with current assumptions. They may even know what really happened. As yet, no one is suggesting Old World contact and trade as the answer—even though I am sure it has occurred to many.

It is evident that many of the controversial, seemingly hard to solve problems in the field of archeology will all quickly be worked out if the new paradigm is accepted. For the last area, Lake Superior, we will again return to the evidence and pull it all together.

8 *Where Does The Evidence Point*

The mines

The mines, our most significant evidence, point to the Minoan traders—the only known group that was searching for copper by sea in 2000 BC. They had the motive, the ability, and in the end, they were the only group that could market vast quantities of North American copper, so that it would essentially disappear from the North American continent. More could be said, but the essential evidence and key to this mystery from the mines is as follows. The volume, once it was removed—much of it in large pieces weighing hundreds or thousands of pounds—had to be smelted. Otherwise, it would still be found somewhere in North America. Twenty to fifty million pounds of copper just does not disappear.

The second key information we get from the mines is the dates. These also point to the Minoan culture. No other culture existed within the time frame of these dates, 2450 BC to 1200 BC, which had the ability or motive to do it. Here is the key to the date evidence. None of the other cultures, like the Egyptians or Assyrians, were effectively destroyed in 1200 BC, signaling the end of the mining related activities in the Wisconsin based archaic Old Copper Complex peoples. The final destruction of the Minoan culture on Crete by the Dorian Greek warlords broke the link to Ugarit and the markets to the east and south. Ugarit itself was also destroyed in this time of upheaval. This caused a chain of actions and reactions that can be followed from the mines back in Wisconsin to New England, Ireland and possibly further. I have not been able to examine the archeological record any further east.

The changes in New England brought to an end the Pre-Algonquin culture. Again, their languages began to diversify into sub-groups. The megalithic group lost its religious center and ceased to exist except locally. This is not as striking, but it is evidence and will be discussed later in the language evidence section.

In Ireland, the archeological record chronicles an influx of new talent, much as you would expect to happen in a colony, when the mother country is destroyed. Some of the refugees would have made their way to the colonies instead of being caught up in the wars of the homeland. These people would have brought their skills and knowledge with them. It would be natural that they would have been working in the metal trades, since that is what these colonies provided. This all happened in 1200 BC when Crete was overrun and the trade stopped.

This sums up the mine evidence. It all strongly points to our Minoan Trade Cartel as the perpetrator.

The Dolmen and Monolithic Stones

The dolmen evidence takes us back to the sun worshiping cultures of Ireland, southern England, and western France. The evidence is not definitive as to which culture, because in each new location the resulting amalgam culture would look different. The adoption of the stone monoliths seems to come from the Old European cultural associations. By 1800 BC when the blue stones were erected at Stonehenge, the trade cartel had a substantial percentage of its members made up of the Maritime Bell-Beaker, or Old European group. What is still present is the Sun-god aspect of these sites. The religious ceremonies connected with the dolmens and standing stones, made the trip all the way to the mines. Many aspects of these religious events can still be found in the Cree and other related nations. The stones themselves just indicate sun worshipers.

The written Ogham evidence on the stones is more controversial. To many, the Ogham script is fact; to others, it is explained away as fanciful theories. I believe the former, that this language is fact. I personally have read the name, "Baal," the sun god of the Canaanites of Ugarit carved on the standing stones and dolmen in the area of the mines, both in Michigan and Minnesota. Therefore, this is strong evidence for either the Minoan or Canaanite traders being here. Recent archeological reports from England have noted the discovery of the tall man sculpture carved into the chalk hills of England. They have shown he carried a skin over his arm. This connects these sculptures, and consequently the monoliths to the male Sun God of the Mediterranean. More and more evidence is showing up that this one powerful God, with so many names in so many cultures, is really one and the same God.

Consequently, in summary I say: The evidence of the dolmens and standing stones carved with the name of "Baal" is potent evidence for the miners being the Minoan trade group and their Ogham using associates from Western Europe.

The Calendar Site

The calendar site is a quite common occurrence in North America. It seems that many of the so-called native tribes used the equinox and summer and winter solstice to mark their religious calendars. We can assume this developed out of a local need to worship on these days, or we can assume that this is a relic of some strongly held religious ceremony of the distant past.

I, for one, believe this is a relic of the Monolithic Sun Worshipping religion. A people, who because of their Neolithic agricultural and sea navigational backgrounds, had a need to know accurate measurements of time. This group believed the great beings of the sky were gods. They had a strong astronomical history and had long ago learned to divide the year by using these heavenly bodies. With these divisions they had learned how to create an accurate solar clock. In some locations they even built their own mountains, because their new country had none. On these high mounds they could honor the Sky Gods and check their cycles. I do not believe these calendars were new creations.

I support the relic theory, that's why I think the calendar is good evidence in support of the Minoan Miners Cartel theory.

Copper Artifact Evidence

Similarities in all the basic copper culture artifacts have always been known—when the European ones were compared to the North American ones, the similarities were obvious. The bulk of the copper culture artifacts give no clue as to who might have done the mining.

The woodworking artifact, heavy axes and wedges like those shown in Graphic's Number 24 and 61, here are artifacts that would have been essential to anyone cutting firewood for mining or for chipping away the stone from the strange red rock called copper. Why would it seem strange for these hunting people to stop carrying these tools after they no longer worked in the mines? It seems only natural to me that they would continue to use clay pots, fishnets, and the light, birch-bark, covered canoes. These would be very helpful. One has to ask, "Who needed to cut firewood, when the woods are full of dry dead trees? Or why should they still have and use the tools, when the men who brought them no longer came for the red copper stones?"

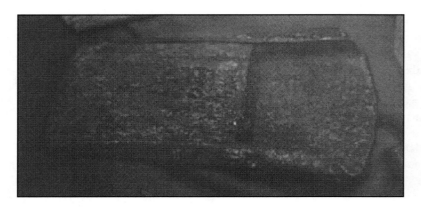

G - 61 Wood Working Tool, Author's Photo

I believe the fact the Old Copper Culture stopped using these tools in 1200 BC indicates that they stopped mining at that time.

Technological Evidence: From the records of the Milwaukee Public Museum and the photos connected to George A West's publication (Ref. No.2). I was able to uncover several very interesting photos that upon close examination should inspire questions to be asked.

G - 62 Blades With Rivet Holes

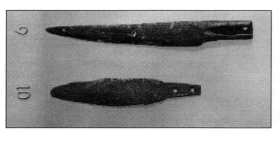

One problem is that several of the blades and points appear to have been fastened to the shafts by rivets or nails. The holes are still very evident. These holes are shown on picture above. The hunter-gather groups in North America did not, to my knowledge, use this technology, but it was being used in the Middle East at the time. Why then, were these artifacts showing up at the Old Copper Culture sites or presumably at the mines themselves? One could well ignore this type of information prior to carbon dating, but now it begs for an answer.

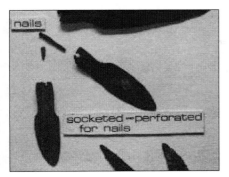

G – 63 Nails for Fasteners

Another Old Copper Site has been discovered at Alpena, Michigan. They have set up a small museum with numerous items in it. In one of the displays, we find this description of nails to hold on spear points, which is more evidence of this technology.

Another of the artifacts appears to be totally different in design. One of the spear points is definitely four-sided. This technical advance was presumably to increase the strength and possibly to pierce armor. This is shown in Photo No. 28. The archeologists make no mention of the change in technology that this point represents.

G - 64 Four-Sided Point, Milwaukee Museum of Natural history

Distribution of Copper artifacts: There is one very complete analysis of the dispersal of copper artifacts; it was written by Ira L. Fogel in September 1963. In this article, Fogel has set apart three time periods—Late Archaic (2200 BC to 1200 BC), Transitional (1400 BC to 800 BC) and Early Woodland (800 BC to 500 AD). These three time periods correspond very closely to the periods I have also discovered. This book is primarily concerned with the Late Archaic period.

Here, we will go to direct quotes. *"For the early phase (*Late Archaic*), no site occurs in Wisconsin or Illinois. Yet Lower Michigan, Ohio, Southern Ontario, and Western New York appear to have been areas of moderate copper artifact density."* (41) p -165

In his article, Fogel indicates, of the 28 artifacts noted they are all found from 300 to 700 miles east of the Keweenaw Peninsula (their source):

> *Projectile points appear to be highly concentrated in Wisconsin with secondary concentrations in Minnesota, Upper Michigan, and Ontario, where as celts and adzes appear to be used during the earlier phases of the Late Archaic in eastern Lower Michigan, eastern Ontario and western New York: and in the later phases in western New York, Wisconsin and Illinois. The tendency for celts and adzes to occur in the more distant reaches of copper distribution is striking.* (41) p - 169

In this one long and confusing sentence, where Fogel has mixed types of artifact, time phases, and numerous locations, he makes a very significant statement. To paraphrase, it should read as: Celts and adzes appear to be used during the early phases of the Late Archaic in eastern Lower Michigan, eastern Ontario, and western New York. He does find this as striking, that these items are found so far from the mines or living area. One could surmise they might have been tools of the boat or ship building trades.

Fogel, although still wordy, comes to an interesting conclusion:

> *The dispersal of copper was similar to that of many other restricted resources in that the center or centers of production and utilization occur at some distance from the source of the raw material. In fact, such long-distance movements of raw material, and finished artifacts, were so common in Late Archaic, Early Woodland, and Middle Woodland times that cultural change and development may have been a partial consequence of inter-regional communication and trade . . . . Further, the difference in regional utilization during the three postulated phases of the Late Archaic suggests that the original development of the copper industry may have occurred some distance east of the latter and better-known Wisconsin centers. This communication* (trade) *was doubtless facilitated by the network of lakes and streams.* (41) p - 170

Part of this could read, that the development of the woodland culture may have been the result of the copper trade. To state this clearly, in 1962, would have brought most careers to an end. No wonder Fogel chose long complicated sentences.

In this fascinating study, we find excellent work with little to no conclusions drawn. For example, if the copper use originated in the east why are there no knives or projectile points in the east? There is, of course, the logical answer for the last sites to be the islands where the St. Lawrence leaves Lake Ontario and heads for the sea. The destination of the copper that went east was not New York. It was simply loaded on ships and sent much further east to Ireland, Spain or Portugal, where it was made into bronze.

Consequently there was no local use of the copper in New York. All that was used there was the celts and adzes of the boat building trade and a few awls to fix their sails. What better place to build and maintain the ships and lake boats than the south shore of Lake Ontario? There were plenty of pine and cedar for the construction ships and boats, and it was only a short trip by light canoe down the Mohawk and Hudson Rivers to their winter home. In these early stages with the strong market, the copper was apparently too valuable to use locally. Besides, the people were primarily fishermen, which were sea-based cultures for which the use of projectile points would be limited.

Here is a very good example where excellent fieldwork and a fair analysis, by a working archeologist, seemed to be used to draw either no conclusion or the wrong conclusions. In all fairness, Fogel probably said as much as he dared. If he had suggested an original copper market east of New York in the 2000 BC period, his article may never have been published.

Yet, what other conclusion can really be drawn? The only Old Copper Culture we are aware of used the knives and spear points at their residence sites. By default, this means the easternmost finds in Ontario and New York could not be residence sites. If they were not residence sites or primary use sites, then these sites must be still further east. All we have further east is the St. Lawrence River and the Atlantic Ocean.

Religious Information: Two artifacts from Michigan and Wisconsin beg comparison with religious items of the Minoan culture. They are shown below. Both the double ax and the snake were very important to the Minoan religious leaders.

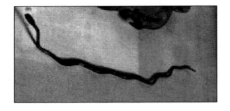

G - 65 Copper Snake, Eastern Mediterranean, Author's Photo

The geologists date the small copper snake, which was recovered from the Nipissing phase beach of glacial Lake Superior, at about 1500 BC. The quality of the workmanship leads one to believe it must have been cast. Closer examination is needed for this. Yet, no one can question its similarity to the ancient Greek snake to which it is compared. Archeologists often discount individual finds like this, because they seem to be out of context. But, really, are they?

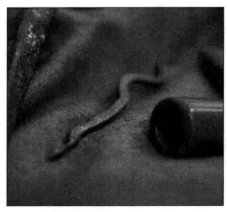

G -66 Copper Snake, Sault Ste. Marie, Ontario, Author's Photo

Here we have a sea people, probably starting to embark on a long, dangerous voyage around the northeast shore of Lake Superior. It is a lake that can snap a 750-foot ore carrier, like the *Edmond Fitzgerald*, in half, just as it did in 1975. It is also a lake, where the safe harbors are few and far between, where the strong westerly winds can smash you into the ever present rocky eastern shore.

It does not seem out of context at all, that we should find a delicate beautiful little snake effigy left on the shore of the last safe harbor, especially when Ishtar was known to be the goddess of the Storms. Ishtar was thought to be able to rise or quiet the storm seas at will. This one small artifact makes a resounding statement about sailors far from home, wise to the risks of Kitchi-Gummi's storms, asking for help on the last leg of a very long and dangerous journey.

The Wisconsin double ax, by now, is probably a ceremonial ornament on a prayer stick or staff, going back some 4000 years, much as shown in this wall fresco from the Minoan city of Knossos.

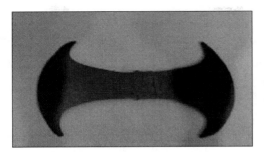

G - 67 Double Ax
Minoan, Author's Photo
Iracklion Museum Crete

Some say the double ax symbol represents the metamorphosis of the butterfly, which is still loved and used by many artists and writers today. This symbol would be very important to some loving devotee, possibly manufactured from a local piece of copper to remind him of some ceremony from home thousands of miles away.

G - 68 Double Ax,
Wisconsin, Ref. (2)

This greenstone artifact, found in the Old Copper Site in Alpena, Michigan, may also be such a symbol. It was displayed as a bannerstone or counter weight used with a spear thrower, but this may or may not be true. The article is quite beautiful to be throwing around in the woods. I think it could just as well be a ceremonial object. In either case, it is just speculation and proves nothing except these people worked the stones they thought of as beautiful.

G 69 Minoan Double Ax on staff,
Authors Photo, Iracklion,
Museum

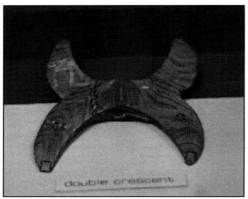

G - 70 Greenstone From Old Copper find in Alpena, Michigan

When our soldiers went off to battle in World War I and II, many a young man kept with him a small cross, a gift from a grandmother or Sunday school teacher of his childhood; we heard stories of how they would hold them on the worst days just to make it through. Why then would we not expect some young Minoan navigator, interpreter, or priest to keep with him the symbols of religious metamorphosis—a belief that the fear and hard work of months or years at sea or mining in a strange land could be transformed into something beautiful in the end. Perhaps, he would remember the beautiful murals painted on the walls of his grandfather's palace back in the homeland he had not seen for three years.

I believe these religious items tell volumes. Both the snake and the double ax point directly to the Minoan Cartel. These religious items, as I have already stated, seemed to have survived the continual watering down of this culture's identity. This probably happened, because it still met the needs of the people. Also, the early Priest-king's agents used religion to forge larger more cohesive groups. To do this, the religion needed to be taught to the new cultures. It could be changed or influenced by the new cultures, but the new amalgam society needed religion to support and provide the essentials for the process to work. The group's moral traits of honesty, loyalty, and dedication must be accepted by the new cultures, if worldwide trade was to prosper. If not, the trade's chain links would have been broken. Therefore, finding the double ax in the Archaic Copper Complex of Wisconsin completes the religious link—just as the copper snake found in the Nipissing beaches near Sault Ste. Marie, Ontario, indicate boatmen still feared the Bull of the Sky that Ishtar could call down.

At the location of the calendar site, 80 miles North of Sault Ste. Marie, there are two other red paint symbols that cause a person to wonder: The first is a painting of boat with a sail and pendant on the top of the mast. The other is "Michipeshu"(some call the great horned lynx), the monster of Lake Superior. It is found along with the representation of two snakes and a canoe or boat. One cannot help but wonder if the horned Michipeshu was just another name for the "Horned Bull of the Sky" in the Gilgamesh tale of 4000 years ago—where Ishtar (the snake) asked to smash Gilgamesh (presumably in his boat).

There are also numerous paintings of horned men at sites according to Thor Conway in his little book (40, P – 17). Are these coincidence or separate inventions? Some of the other Red Indian paintings represent the zodiac symbols. I have not used these symbols as hard evidence since they are not dated, but they must be mentioned if one is to get the whole story of the Lake Superior copper area. Was the Maritime Archaic Red Paint Culture just another name for the Amalgam culture of the Minoan traders and the Algonquin speaking locals?

G - 71 Michipeshu,
Author's Photo

If so, did the horns of consecration also survive the trip half-way around the world? Are the Viking horns and the sacred buffalo horns of the Black Feet and Teton Sioux used and honored in the same fashion as horns worn by the attacking sea people that are so clearly shown on the walls of tombs of Egypt? This kind of evidence will be called supposition by many, and rightly so. Yet, the snake and the double ax cannot be so identified. They are here, and they point to one group, the Minoans.

Miscellaneous Evidence and Questions: There are three bits of evidence that need to be mentioned if only in passing. They are not direct Wisconsin evidence but relate instead to general trade between the New World and the Old world three to four thousand years ago. In 1977 a French scientist, named Dr. Michelle Lescot, while working with the mummy of Ramses II found tobacco in some of his body cavities. Tobacco is a plant that is supposed to be only found in the Americas. Later another scientist from Germany, Dr. Svetla Balabnova, while doing tissue analysis on Egyptian mummies, found traces of cocaine in their bodies; cocaine is also an American plant. This is solid evidence for trade. (This will be expanded in the Epilog)

Pottery is often used as a base line for dating information by many archeologists. Therefore the information is carefully recorded. Two quotes from James H. Kellar, archaeologist for the Indiana Historical Society and Director of Glenn A. Black Laboratory of Archaeology, have significance on this subject. He is writing about the woodland tradition in his little book, *An Introduction to the Prehistory of Indiana.*

The woodland tradition is basically defined by the presence of pottery containers with surfaces distinguished by cord impressions or other decorations applied using a flat paddle-like tool.

The origin of pottery in northeastern North America is presently unclear. The oldest pottery in North America was made in Georgia - Florida area at about 2,000 BC. It is thick, heavy, and tempered with vegetable fiber.

Because cord-impressed pottery is also an Old World characteristic, it has been proposed that this idea was introduced from there into the New World, either from northeast Asia or Europe. Logical as this might appear at first view, the simple fact is that thousands of miles intervene between the two distributional areas with no direct evidence to connect them. (48) p - 35

This well informed professional is telling us, the jury is still out on the introduction of pottery in the northeastern United States. He is also saying the logical answer is not being considered, because the distances seem to far. The thousands of miles "*with no direct evidence*" are oceans. What type of evidence would we be looking for in the ocean? Both of these questions, the introduction timing, and the cord impressed styles fit perfectly and support our theory.

So, the hard, copper artifact, evidence resoundingly points to the Minoan trade group and their associates from Western Europe. The soft evidence points to a culture that used the zodiac symbols and represented the sacred horns as part of their religious beliefs. Also, this is a good fit for the Minoan culture. And finally some un-answered questions seem to be looking for just such an answer.

Yet, there is more. It is the written material we have classed as the language evidence covered in the next chapter.

9 Language and Other Evidence

The reader has a right to stop me here and say, "Yes, this is all interesting, but what really ties it all together? Why should I believe that these Minoan priest kings or their cartel members were really the ones who came over here and did the mining? Yes, the time is right; yes, the motive was there, and they definitely had the ability, but I need more."

I am now going to again mention Dr. Barry Fell and the work of his "Epigraphic Society." I have purposefully not quoted Dr. Fell's books extensively, so that I might show the evidence is there with or without his work. I do, however, believe he is one of the true fathers of this theory. Although I was only able to talk to him once on the phone before he died, I respect and admire his work. He has been ridiculed by "nit-pickers" for his minor omissions and errors, but this can be expected by anyone who sets out to correct significant errors of the establishments in power.

Regardless of all this, I am now going to quote Dr. Fell, since he actually has studied one of my most significant pieces of evidence, "The Newberry Tablet" as he calls it. When he did this interpretation, no one had located the original newspaper article from Newberry, Michigan, or the original photos that had been sent to the Smithsonian Institute back in 1896. They were not lost; no one had looked for them. I am not sure if he was made aware of these findings before he died, but I am sure it would have been of great interest to him.

The Newberry Tablet is a key document in this discussion. The fact that it existed cannot be questioned. The fact as to its authenticity, although questioned by some, appears to be very solid. Therefore, Dr. Fell's interpretation of it as written history is extremely important.

Below is a quote from the first four paragraphs of his article as it appeared in the June 1981, *Occasional Publication of The Epigraphic Society*, Vol. 9 No. 218. The article is titled, *"Decipherment and Translation of the Newberry Tablet From Northern Michigan."*

As reported by Dr. Henriette Mertz in the preceding article, a drawing was sent to me by Dr. Mertz, at my request, showing the form and arrangement of the symbols observed on the ceramic tablet when it was excavated. I informed Dr. Mertz that the syllabary, for such it is, a variant of the well-known Cypro-Minoan script, comprised an omen text, similar to that of the

Phaistos Disk (OPES vol. 4). The language comprising the text appears to be a creolinized form of Minoan, having a vocabulary similar to that of Hittite, but lacking the formal declensions and conjugations of Hittite.

The vocabulary of this American omens text from Michigan invites comparison with that of the Cherokee (an Algonquian) *language as well as with that of the Linear A tablets of Crete, and the Phaistos Disk.*

The syllabary of the tablet has already (OPES vol. 8) been compared with other known Cypro-Minoan syllabaries, and requires no further discussion here.

The contained vocabulary is given in full later in this paper. A sample of the similarities of the vocabulary to the other languages I have just named may be illustrated by these examples. (42) p - 132

One further quotation for many readers who may wish to know is this: *"The Hittite-Minoan roots can all be found in Sturtevant's or Friedrich's Hittite Dictionaries, as already described in detail in the various papers already published in OPES vol 4." (42) p - 135*

G - 72 Sample Syllabary Sketch (RJ) Ref. (44) p - 158

I have included a sample syllabary above so that you may better understand what Dr. Fell is referring to in this discussion.

Without trying to become an expert on ancient texts or asking my readers to do so, we have here a document (The Newberry Tablet) that ties the Minoan civilization to the copper mines of Lake Superior. It is, if you will, an virtual fingerprint at the scene of the action. People think through their language. The Minoan language, found at the source of the copper in Michigan, is as good as DNA. The fact that the language has been modified over time is also important. It means this tablet was not just brought here, but could only be created from years of using the syllabary.

It also ties the Minoan culture to that of the Hittite, something that many other writers have hinted at, but up until this time, had no concrete proof. It also implies a long-lasting relationship with natives in this country that can still be found 4000 years later in the Cherokee Nation (Probable Adena descendants).

Dr. Fell's Credibility: It is because of the enormous impact his words imply, that Dr. Fell's is so often berated. It is easier to kill the messenger than to deal with the message. However, not all archeologists are so quick to condemn. D. H. Kelly published an article in the prestigious *Review of Archaeology*, Volume 11, Number 1, Spring 1990. Although he does point out Fell's shortcomings, the entire article is a must read for anyone who would render an opinion on Dr. Fell's work. I have included a few quotes for your consideration.

> *With respect to the Old World, he has proffered a very substantial number of decipherments of texts which have been previously unread. The scripts of Mohenjodaro, the Phaistos disc, Minoan Linear "A", Etruscan, two languages written in Libyan (Numidian), the Paphian-Cypriote syllabary, Basque, Micronesian, Easter Island, and a considerable number of others are presented, usually in full translation (the one clear mark of an amateur in his work). . . ."Although I do not yet have firm opinions on many of these decipherments, I am convinced that they are all to be taken seriously. (45) p - 3*

There is another section in Kelly's article about Fell that is key to this work. We have pointed out, that on two monolithic structures, the Ogham words of B-L have been found. Kelly addresses the use of Ogham in North America:

> *Another sequence which recurs several times in Colorado and New England (and once, as Leonard has pointed out, in Scotland) is B-L, Bel, Beli, the name of the sun god associated particularly with the Irish festival of Beltane. . . . The most striking thing about it was the letters B-L set into a cube drawn in perspective, bisected by a shadow cast by the setting equinoctial sun. . . . The name Ogum corresponds to that of the Gaulish god of eloquence, Ogmious, equivalent to the Gaelic Ogma Sun-face, a sun god and the mythical inventor of the Ogham script, named after him. The name is entirely appropriate to a site, which contains numerous solar alignments.* (45) p - 7,8

Although it is not indicated here, the sun god of the Irish 'Bel' is the same as the Canaanite sun god, 'Baal'.

> *Despite my occasional harsh criticism of Fell's treatment of individual inscriptions, it should be recognized that without Fell's work, there would be no Ogham problem to perplex us. We need to ask not only what Fell has done wrong in his epigraphy, but also where we have gone wrong as archeologist in not recognizing such an extensive European presence in the New World. (45) p-10*

The Newberry Tablet, Real or Fake

The establishment detractors usually say the Newberry Tablet is all faked, faked by loggers from a small town in northern Michigan who probably had little or no education. I will now present more on the truth of this discovery from investigators at the time.

Some local people of the time also considered the possibility of a fake, so a party of four of the area's more learned men:

> *". . . consisting of Dr. H. C. Farrand, Messrs: W.T. Crocker, D. N. McLeod, Wm. Trueman, and Charles Brebner, drove out to the place where the find was made with the intention of doing a little exploring. They found the upturned hemlock root where the figures and the tablet were dug out, but owing to recent thaws, the hole was filled with water. . . . several test pits were sunk and rock was struck every time and the party was of the opinion that further important discoveries would yet be made. (46) Hospital Edition 571.*

The article from the *Mining Journal*, a paper from Marquette, Michigan, about 50 miles west of the find, goes on to show pictures of two of the statues and the tablet. It connects the mining to the mound culture of which much evidence was being uncovered daily as the farmers opened up new fields in other parts of Michigan. They, of course, did not know of the carbon dating time difference between this culture and the Isle Royal mines in 1896.

We also have a letter written May 12, 1958 by M. B. Fritz, editor and publisher of *The Newberry News* to the Marquette Historical Society. In this letter, Mr. Fritz is quoting information given to him by his father, William G. Fritz—presumably the paper's editor in 1896. He states the following:

> *The images were found on Robert McGruer's forty-acre parcel four miles north of town, in a comparatively shallow depression under the roots of an uprooted hemlock tree. The lot was brought to town and a great hassle arose concerning them, which has not yet been settled. Some investigation was made by the parties you name, pictures sent to the Smithsonian Institute, but they could tie it up with nothing in history known at the time. Dr. Farrand, Crocker, McLeod, Trueman and Brebner were all intelligent men, but one or two of them were prone to rig up practical jokes, and town opinion was about equally divided as to whether they really had something, or were just giving the cracker box boys something to chew on. Father was of the opinion they were sincere, that the find was no joke. One of his reasons that McGruer was a rather simple minded old coot with no capacity for such a stunt, and, when properly lubricated, told all he knew anyway. Father lubricated him, but got nothing more than the facts stated. Since McGruer made the find while clearing land, he must have been a charter member of the affair, whatever it was.*
> *(47)*

This was located in private correspondence from M. F. Fretz to Kenyon Boyer managing director of the Marquette Historical Society, May 12, 1958. Mr. Fretz, also goes on to give his personal firsthand knowledge of the find:

> *As a young boy on my way to the swimming hole on the Tahquamonon River, I remember those figures being stored in an open wagon shed on the McGruer farm on the river. Somewhere in my musty old files I have pictures of them. My impression is*

that they were not made of sandstone, but of red clay, baked hard, with some kind of surfacing. The molded figures were very roughly made, but obviously human beings. There were three of them, about four, three, and two feet in height.

The tablet at the time I saw it, about 1905 or 1906, was beginning to disintegrate from exposure and being kicked around, and was formed of the same reddish material as the figures. The characters meant nothing to a 10 or 11 year-old kid, but a number of years later I saw the tablet, and the characters impressed me as being wedge shaped, like a Persian cuneiform tablet, but these were separated by squares. In no manner did they resemble Greek, Egyptian, or any other ancient tablet writing, but of course my ignorance far exceeds my knowledge in that field. (47)

Fingerprints at the scene: But now, we must get back to our proof. Here our goal is simple. We just want to know, "Who did the mining?" This piece of evidence, "The Newberry Tablet," as interpreted by Fell, is similar to the famous leather glove dropped by Mr. Simpson in the greatest murder trial of this century. If we could somehow reason the glove was planted, we could let our old hero go free. For the same reason, the establishment proclaimed the Newberry Tablet was planted, so we could continue to live with our comfortable old assumptions. It worked for Mr. Simpson and for 100 years, it has worked for the old archeologist establishment. The real trouble is, in my opinion, the public did not buy the Simpson story, and they no longer are going to buy the planted Newberry Tablet theory either.

Jim Guthrie, an excellent researcher in the NEARA group, recently did an analysis of the symbol pairs on the tablet. His findings were that there were far too many pairs and groups of symbols for their arrangement to be random. His conclusion was there is a high probability the Newberry Tablet is made up of words and phrases.

Considering the evidence that still exists and the eyewitness statements of the time, I believe we must conclude the Newberry Tablet was, in fact, no hoax. I believe it was only the "elitist arrogance" of a few people of that time that caused these beautiful relics, probably 4000 years old, to be nearly lost to us.

After much thought, I believe the following probably occurred. The baked clay statues and text had been in the sand for so many centuries, that the locals believed them to be sandstone. At first, this gave me a problem, but now I realize the sand had probably chemically adhered to the clay figures, making them appear as sandstone. The existing remnants, of the figures I found are definitely baked clay.

This Cypriot Tablet shown below of the same period compares very favorably also with the Newberry Tablet. It was from a Tell in the eastern Mediterranean and was photographed in a British museum by the author. Several symbols are exactly the same.

G - 73 Cypriot Tablet, from a tell in the Mediterranean Area, Author's Photograph

The facts I have uncovered in this personal investigation indicate the tablet is not a fake. The error was made by the intellectuals of the period who, in 1896, dismissed these artifacts as the creations of a local hoax. Dr. Fell is probably very close to correct in his theory and interpretation about the tablet. This error would not be so bad if it was not still being promoted by some in the establishment today. The photos I used came out of a folder in the Smithsonian Institute labeled "Michigan Fakes".

With this, I think we can put to rest the idea that the Newberry Tablet and "McGruer's Gods" were faked. In doing this, we now have in our hands a piece of written Minoan history right here on Lake Superior, less than a hundred miles from the copper mines. This is, however, not the only language evidence.

The Sutton, New Hampshire Land Deed: As we pointed out in the earlier evidence section, we still must deal with the Sutton, New Hampshire Land Deed. New Hampshire is blessed with many monolithic stone structures, so it should be no surprise that this is where this second piece of language evidence also turns up. We again turn to Dr. Barry Fell to see why we have chosen this particular evidence.

A reprint of, *The Sutton Historical Society Bulletin,* Vol. VI No 4 December 1980, is readily available. Yet, what needs to be said is this:

> *The Sutton Deed is signed by the Indian owners of the land, they used two different alphabets. . . . Those who preferred to use the ancient Algonquin writing system signed their names in a form of script called Mamalohikin, in which the letters stand for individual syllables, and the letters themselves are those of the ancient alphabet of Cyprus. The Cypriot inscriptions on the Island of Cyprus remained indecipherable until 1871. (10) EPSOP Vol. 13 no. 313*

Here again, we have the Cypro-Minoan script being used by a group of Algonquin speaking natives long after it should have disappeared. This strengthens the long-term nature of this early contact and, as the facts reveal, it is found along the "Tracks in Stone" route. However, now, it is on this side of the Atlantic.

Let's return to the question at hand. We know the mines were created. Physical and empirical time frame evidence makes the Minoan/ Cypriot/ Hittite Cartel a strong suspect. Now we have two far separated sources of written historical fact that state they were, in fact, here. The language is equivalent to actual fingerprints at the scene. One source is at, the site of the mines; the other is at the probable over-winter site. The Language appears to be rock hard evidence the mining was done by the Minoans.

The Creation Of Syllabaries: As stated earlier in Chapter 6, "The People," did these ancient Minoan traders actually write down the languages of their various trading partners or colonies as they moved out across the world? It seems the evidence concurs that this is exactly what was done. The connection of the ancient Basque alphabet with the Cree alphabet, as pointed out by Dr. Fell in the Sutton Land Deed paper seems to also substantiate this.

I need to digress a bit here to point out some key elements in the Cree language and the syllabary in which it is written. In 1988, I found myself the Fire Camp Boss on a fire on the "Rocky-Boy Indian Reservation" in Montana. These Chippewa and Cree people had been relocated to this reservation in the 1800s. A Cree woman, named Harriet Standing Rock, was on my office staff. When she heard I was writing a book that would incorporate some of Dr. Fell's work, she volunteered to write down the Cree alphabet for me. I still have the original today.

She said I could learn it quickly because it was just the consonants turned to the four directions. Example:

La le li lo,
pa pe pi po,
ma me mi mo,

At the time, I did not fully assimilate what she was saying, for my mind was on other things. The fire was still raging. However, later with considerable study of an old copy of the syllabary, I was able to see how one symbol was simply rotated to the four directions to convey the full meaning including the vowels. As an example of this:

< pa V pe ∧ pi > po

Upon close examination, it is obvious that the symbols of this syllabary system were carefully designed for quick writing, possibly with a stylus on clay. The idea that the vowels were implied is not really true here, if the context of the writing is known. For example, if the lines are horizontal with the top representing north—the entire meaning of the syllabary chart can convey, both consonants and vowels.

The syllabary form of writing is quite simple and could, no doubt, be learned quickly. The sounds of any spoken language could simply be recorded on clay for the primary words necessary to conduct the trade. Once recorded on a comparative clay text (dictionary if you will), it could be studied and used for centuries. One key here is obvious. The trader apparently adjusted to the environment of "the new language" in the area he was trading. With some coaching by the scholars, a young merchant's scribe could know the basic language before he set foot in a new land, providing they had been there before and were able to record the basic vocabulary. This utilized skills that were abundant in the primary trade center of Ugarit.

It is obvious that a learned culture could easily spread the use of such a basic syllabary along their trade routes, but it takes a lot of wild speculation to invent a theory of how these separate syllabaries could have been created independently. It is this historic movement of a basic written syllabary along the Tracks in Stone Trade Route that helped me develop my final theory about the event. It is fascinating to imagine how the old Linear "A & B" syllabaries of the Cypriot /Minoan traders, when numbered or charted, became the source for the ancient Basque alphabet, then the Ogham script of the Druids, the Runic script of the ancient Vikings, and finally, the source for the Cree and Cherokee syllabaries.

To some, this may in itself take a giant leap of faith, but when the Ogham characters and the runic characters are thought of as simple numbers on a chart, it becomes quite feasible. I believe that linguists will be able to see these relationships, if they look. For all I know, maybe they already have. These languages may not all represent the same exact syllabic chart, since there is a significant spread of time here, and of course, some of the languages would have had very different sounds. However, the technology of the writing and translation should be the same.

There is one other point to mention. Many of the unrelated languages, Etruscan, Basque, and Algonquin, would all have been original primitive languages of the area. It was only by a twist of fate that these were recorded with the flexible Minoan syllabary and, eventually, became an enigma to subsequent scholars.

It is sufficient for this study to be able to say that the people at the mine site, "The Cree," and the people at the smelting center, "The Basque," used the same alphabet (syllabary). One other point can be made. New words, not found in the existing local languages, may be the same in the revised languages along the route. This might explain some of the similar words in the Finnish and Algonquian languages. This is just a thought. I am not a linguist.

As a side note, it is interesting that members of the Cree nation still carry family names like Standing Rock (very monolithic) and Sun Child (very sun worship related). Also, they still have, in their syllabary, a symbol that stands for equinox that looks just like the ancient calendar site—Eye of God Symbol. I am sure there are members of this great nation who could shed much light on this, if they so chose. I am not sure, however, that they will trust us enough to do it. They do not need to have their history trivialized or their sacred languages more desecrated. After all, it is our view of history that needs to be changed, not theirs.

I know this is not hard evidence that the "Cree" Nation embodies in part the essence of the "Cretan" traders who were trapped here in 1200 BC, when the Dorian Greeks destroyed their home office. However, it is my personal belief that a bright young Cree scholar will someday work out the connection, whatever it is.

New Language Evidence:

As I was re-examining the material provided to me by James Guthrie, I noticed a small paper I had missed in the first examination. It was an article written by J. Peter Denny, exploring connections between the Algonquin languages, the Salishan language, and the archeological traditions of record. The paper was published in Ottawa, Canada in 1989 by Carlton University. The article was so interesting it would have been nice to include it all here, but of course, that is not possible. To summarize, Mr. Denny was trying to find an archeological tradition that would explain the very unusual word development he had uncovered in the Cree-Montagnais and Ojibway languages. A few direct quotes from Mr. Denny is the most appropriate way to present this here since the words are quite technical and I may misinterpret something:

> *It was semiotic problems that first made me wonder about the complexities of Algonquin history. I encountered a number of morphemes whose meanings seemed improbable, if it were true that Algonquin speakers had always lived in small hunting bands like those of the Cree-Montagnais and Ojibway speakers in the boreal forest. Some of the puzzles are these: (1) Proto-Algonquian (PA) *elenyiwa 'person' may come from the root *'elenordinary'; this suggests a possibility that ordinary people were contrasted with higher status people in a stratified society at some time earlier in Algonquin history. (43) P-86*

This type of statement clearly relates to the questions I am raising in this text. Did the early Native American groups that everyone agrees were in the area-mining, act alone, or were they being hired or directed by someone who was there to procure the copper?

> *These many morphological identities make it likely that it originally had an instrumental meaning. Its present meaning in both languages is send chase someone', but a hint of its original meaning is seen in the derived nouns I have listed for 'messenger' and 'message'. Its original instrumental meaning must have been 'to do something to someone by sending', i.e., it was an instrumental verb final of sending. It seems unlikely that a culture would develop such a specialized instrumental verb unless doing things by sending others was quite common. It looks again as if some high status people had authority over others. In the egalitarian society of the boreal forest this meaning was lost and the morpheme came to mean just send 'someone'.*

> *3). . . oxkye:wa 'he works' may be related to verbs for hiring and commissioning work. For example, in Ojibway only vowel*

length separates anokki: 'he works' from ano:kki: 'he commissions
something to be done' which is related to ano:n 'to hire someone'
. . . again, this sort of finding suggests a ranked society in the
Algonquin past, in which so much important work was done for
those in authority that the ordinary word meaning 'work' was
derived from those referring to authoritarian control of work. (43)
p - 87

Remember, earlier in the book we said the use of the word, "messenger," would be explained. Well, this is it. Here the word, "messenger", the "seal carrier," so common in the early Mediterranean contracts, was called a messenger of the merchant king. This word seems also to have been used very extensively in the Cree word structure. The words, "hire" and "work," also stand out as non-fitting concepts for the small tribal groups, the structure of which, we are told, the Cree functioned in at that time. They appear to come, instead, from a hierarchical society, for which we have no accepted archeological tradition.

Before we get too far into Mr. Denny's article, we should note that he introduces the concept of an earlier source for all the Algonquian languages. He calls this language, Proto-Algonquian, a source language that can explain some of these unusual word development patterns in the more recent descendent languages.

It is also interesting to look at the specific words Denny finds as his examples. One was, "stones and big stones." Another was, "strings and rope." Both of these words may likely have been introduced by our monolithic sailors who may not have found suitable words in the hunter/gathering languages to communicate about their joint work projects, especially tasks like dragging and erecting huge monolithic boulders.

In the section of his article, labeled "New Theory", Denny states the following: "*We are looking for an archeological tradition of the early woodland period (1500-200 BC) which might be the carrier of the Proto-Algonquian language as it spread out and differentiates into the Al-gonquian languages.*" He has considered both the Red Ocher and Glacial Kame culture, in which I think he meant to include the Adena.

In the section, "Eastern Algonquian", we find the following statement:

Red Ocher, Glacial Kame and Adena heartland on the Scioto
account for the Algonquian expansion into the lower four Great
Lakes. But to account for the Eastern Algonquian languages, from

the Maritimes to Chesapeake Bay requires further explanations.
The crucial area is Southern New England: this is likely to be the
Proto-Algonquian homeland because many more of the
descendent languages are located there than to the north or south.
(43) p - 96

Here we have a startling statement coming from a totally new and different source that says the probable homeland for Proto-Algonquian speech is southern New England. This is the exact same location that the New England Antiquities Research Association (NEARA) reported they have documented hundreds of stone and monolithic structures. The very same place that I contend in my theory, where the Minoan traders began their travel into the copper mines of Lake Superior, and the same place the Tinkham cultures started storing grain in 2400 BC.

It appears that if, in fact, the Minoan trade cartel already operating through Spain and Ireland did set up a trading center in southern New England, it would explain many of Mr. Denny's questions. If they proceeded to hire and work with the indigenous Proto-Algonquian people, it would also explain many of the unanswered questions of NEARA, as to who constructed all those stone monuments. Some of the questions of the New England archeologists, about the beginning of the woodland cultures in that area, would also be answered by this theory. It could help to explain why the Cree and ancient Basque have the same syllabary. It would be another piece in the puzzle as to how the mines on Lake Superior were made, and where the copper might have gone.

Yet, I am not through with Mr. Denny's great work. He indicates the source for the consistent influence and long-time spread of this language was the Adena Culture. I think he is right. My work has led me to believe that in, 1200 BC, when the Minoan trade link was disrupted by the destruction of the main office in Crete and/or Ugarit, the market dried up. This left some of those associated traders, the leaders, lieutenants, princes, etc. stranded in North America.

The situation was ripe for setting up a more authoritarian culture right here on the North America continent (Turtle Island) with these local leaders at its head. It would be a culture organized around some religious rights and with ceremonies to mark the sun's extremes and its seasons. The Serpent Mound and other sites would be their sacred places. They had already been here for over a thousand years. There was most certainly a core group or tribe that was a blending of both those traders who settled here, and the indigenous people who invited them into their homes and villages. I believe this group was the Adena people.

In Mr. Denny's overview, near the end of his article, he put it this way:

> *The spread of Proto-Algonquian, eventuating in its separation into the descendant languages, appears to have been the result of the spread of religious practices by the Red Ocher and Glacial Kame traditions. Starting about 1500 BC - 1200 BC from focus in the Illinois - Wabash regions, these mortuary traditions carried a package of new religious, social, and economic ideas north up both coasts of Lake Michigan, and northeast along the north shore of Lake Erie and Lake Ontario as far as Lake Champlain. The attraction of these new practices probably encouraged bilingualism in the Proto-Algonquian language, which is hypothesized to have been spoken by their originators (for whom no archeological identity is yet established). (43)*

Mr. Denny's work clearly defines the route of the miners west from southern New England, west to Lake Champlain and on to Lake Superior. The 1500 BC date is right for the movement into the Mississippi River Valley with the close of the Ottawa due to up lift. Site along the Mississippi and Arkansas River also support his premise.

I really must compliment Mr. Denny on his work. I was thrilled at how accurately his theories on the development of these languages fit into my theories on the miners of Lake Superior copper. All my work does is provide the reason and destination locations supporting the movements he describes and the probable cultural changes that he believed took place. Mr. Denny has clearly shown consequence in the Cree language that can well be explained by my theory of trade.

Summary:

I believe the objectives I had set out in the foreword have been met. A solid case has been presented that a second culture was involved in the mining of the ancient copper mines of Lake Superior. If this is accepted as fact, then several additional questions must be asked. Did this contact result in the beginnings of the woodland culture? Did this and other trade contracts cause the Native American language diversity? Should we move away from the concept of grouping all native language groups to-gether, as Native American studies, and create a real area of studies called Ancient American History? It seems that we owe this to ourselves as Americans.

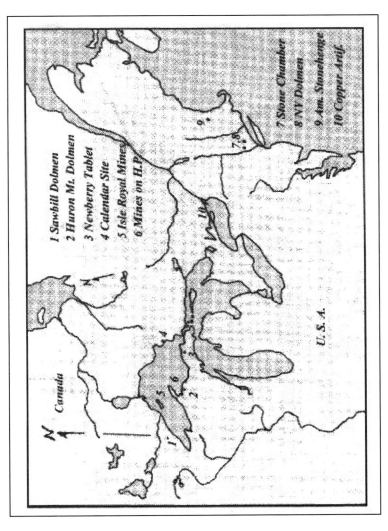

G - 74 Map of Hard Evidence Sites,
Sketch by author

10 New Ancient American History

I have provided you the reader with the facts as I've found them: First, the uncontested information that the mines did and actually do exist. Second, that most of the mines were actually created between 2450 BC and 1200 BC. I have also provided several specific pieces of hard evidence—by no means all that exist. To quickly review, several dolmen in the mining area, and copper artifacts relate to woodworking and ancient religions. The written testimony of many learned and published professionals also supports the theory. This is about as far as one can go in a little book.

Now, I would like to provide what I believe to be a realistic theory as to what really did happen 4000 years ago here on the shores and islands of Lake Superior (Kitchi-Gummi). You, the reader, are in effect, the jury. It will be up to you as to whether or not this controversy continues, or if a new more accurate history is written.

About 6000 years ago, the agricultural revolution began to develop in the eastern end of the Mediterranean. This was not restricted to the two areas we often think of as Egypt and Mesopotamia. It had spread well into the Anatolian peninsula and had already spread by sea to islands in the Aegean Sea and possibly much farther. At first, these cultures embraced the old Mother Goddess religion as was so well defined by Marjorie Gimbus. They were far from Stone Age people. They developed many of the technological advances so important to us today. This is not to say that these advances did not spread from Egypt or Mesopotamia. That is for others to determine. It needs to be understood that much technology already existed over a large area.

This technology included the raising and breeding of cattle and other live stock, and the use of many specially food plants, most probably hybridized accidentally through seed-source selection, and then growing them together in the same field. Weaving was probably known in most areas, and when the villages were near water, the use of boats was probably significant. These boats were probably used for fishing, trading, and resettlement. After all, the new agricultural revolution would have created a population boom. Resettlement and expansion is done by all successful species.

It was within this larger context that we see in about 3500 BC the development of urban centers. It follows then, that shipping and trading lead to the establishment of urban centers, not the other way around.

Many writers and researchers point out that the use of boats or small ships seems to be well under way much before 3000 BC. By 2800 BC, they are already over 100 feet long. It is also clear that enough trade existed for technology of the time to quickly spread. The early Mother Goddess religion must have, in some way, created an environment where sharing and trade blossomed. As the urban centers developed, however, the power and wealth started to concentrate in the two developing areas or nations, if you will.

It is this world in which we find the development of the priest-king city-state traders. They seemed to have come out of the pre-Phoenician Canaanite old Sumerian culture. They blended into what might be called the Neolithic Old European Goddess Culture. This match worked well for both. The small Neolithic villages could not support the creation of high technology—glass, and metal working skills. The economy of scale took over, and the first Industrial Revolution was underway.

In about five hundred years, or we might say fifteen generations, at least by 2500 BC, this system had spread all the way to Britain and Ireland. By now, it had fully integrated the concept of colonization to expand the trade base and, at the same time, allow for the expansion of the now much richer trading families. The normal procedure is well known later in 500 BC in the Phoenician culture, when as many as 60 ships with 30,000 settlers were sent out from Carthage to settle or trade.

Let's not get ahead of ourselves though. By 2500 BC, the traders found and were exploiting the copper and tin resources of both the Iberian Peninsula and the Tin Isles (Britain). First, it would have been lieutenants or "seal carriers" with two or three ships. Then, some of the men would have stayed and married into the local population of Neolithic farmers, if there was a local group. If not, a son of a prominent family member would recruit a settlement force and set up a new little kingdom, such as happened in Northern Ireland.

If I had to give a name to this group that would be recognized by archeologists, it would probably be the Marine Bell-Beaker group. However, this is quite hazardous, because the resulting community would look different if there was or was not a preexisting culture at the new site. This can be seen in the differences between Britain, where there was an existing culture, and Northern Ireland, where there was not. Consequently, in the area where we have new settlements, as in Ireland, the artifact history tells more.

There is a possibility the Hebrides Islands on the northwest coast of Scotland, may well have gotten their name from the Hebernites of Anatolia. Only later would the name be associated with the word hibernation, meaning to winter-over, to some North Sea sailors. The final use of the word, hibernate, is to sit down in their pit homes and wait for spring.

For these reasons, the dates of the establishment of the solar sites at New Grange in Ireland are more important to the mines in the United States than Stonehenge, which is related to the tin mines of Britain. Probably, sailors exploring in and around the Tin Isles, either spotted Iceland or were caught in a storm and blown west across to Iceland, Greenland, and finally Newfoundland on the North American continent. It must be remembered that the priest-king who found the Tin Mines of Britain, became a very rich man. He would not have stopped looking. It is for this reason, I believe, that the New Grange group was first established. It probably was to fully investigate Ireland's resources and explore to the north and west. The copper resources of Ireland and Britain were used in this period.

This enterprising family was well rewarded, because it is evident they must have made the crossing and stumbled on to the richest natural copper ore body in the world. The stimulus of this find allowed for the development of two of the most sophisticated monolithic religious sites in the world, Stonehenge and New Grange. I believe this was probably about the time of the Wessex culture. This kind of copper resource would have been well supported by the home office in Crete or Ugarit. We can think of this as the industrial family "Don" or Senior King.

The resource was too big and important to leave it up to the local hunter-gathering natives to develop. Therefore, a new group was set up in this new land. It was centered in what we now call New England. On the north side, it was an easy trip up the Trent or Ottawa Rivers to the mines on Lake Superior, and on the south and east it provided a better climate to winter-over with a lot of good fishing. The local tribes up around the lake were incorporated into the mining process. The new technologies and easier lifestyles were enough to win over the support and change the locals of southern New England forever. Cloth, blankets, fishnets, bows and arrows, improved boats, pottery, and agriculture changed the local lifestyle so much in the vicinity of the coastal areas that a new culture was born. The first stages of the Early Woodland culture were created. Although I believe an actual settlement took place in New England, it is hard to say what percentage of the population may have been new and what percentage were locals.

Recent genetic work with the new Mitochondria DNA study has discovered a very early X Gene that appears to come from Europe. The work is not final yet but it would be interesting if the X Genes were also prevalent in the Welsh, Cornish and Basque groups. Some Algonquin groups have as high as 25% of this gene. This is much higher than would be expected. One will have to wait for the final proof, but I expect it will indicate that at least 5 or 6 thousand years ago, groups traveled along the ice from Europe to North America. Definitely by 4500 years, the trade existed.

It is obvious that although the Wisconsin tribes probably traded labor for cloth, dyes, fishnets, and other technology when the miners left the locals returned to their original hunting and gathering ways. Yet, life was much easier with the important new technologies.

The culture, that developed with its center in New England presumably traversed back and forth on the St. Lawrence, up the Trent and Ottawa Rivers and down into Lake Superior. At the very earliest time, the Ottawa River was the primary river drain of the Lake Superior Basin. Geological uplift has since changed this. It is doubtful that the actual copper would ever have been taken down into New England. The oceangoing vessels would have actually been taken into the lake or met with somewhat smaller boats along the St. Lawrence. The findings at Peterbourgh seem to support this second theory. These findings also document the fact that these ships were sometimes multi-national or, at least, subcontractors.

Fogel's article on distribution of copper artifacts indicates, the islands on the east end of Lake Ontario were the farthest east copper celts and adzes were found. This fits the scenario perfectly. (41)

Others may have gone north by way of James Bay and Hudson Bay, then east into the North Atlantic. This might have been the original route of discovery. It is obvious that goods moved from one support site to another. For example, movement was from Lake Superior to the St. Lawrence, the St. Lawrence to New Grange, New Grange to Spain (maybe Cadiz), Spain to Sardinia, Sardinia to Crete, Crete to Ugarit, and Ugarit to Egypt or Mesopotamia.

It is possible that the same ship made the whole trip, but it is also possible local captains may have re-negotiated trade goods at every stop. There is no way to tell from the evidence. All we can say for sure is that the copper traveled one way along the tracks in Stone Route, while technology, culture, religion, and writing traveled the other. It is evident that some of these traders and their lieutenants made the whole route, but we cannot really say how many.

It is my personal opinion that enough of these traders were brought here as settlers to totally overpower the existing cultures in the Northeast. The fact that the written language survived in the more ancient form along with a substantial part of the technology is a testament to this. The fact, that the Algonquian Nations in the area adopted a new language without the benefit of war or the change of the people, also supports this.

The destruction of the Minoan home office in Crete and Ugarit in 1200 BC and the resulting forced migration had several repercussions. First, the markets of Egypt and Mesopotamia were cut off. In some areas, iron was replacing bronze. Many Minoan craftsmen moved out along the "Tracks in Stone Trail" from Corfu all the way to Ireland. In Ireland, the archeological record even recorded this influx of new talent.

It is also my personal belief, that the Algonquian language group embodies most of this early group. However, some part of the later trade group that was trapped here in 1200 BC, I believe, went on to organize and become the original mound builders (The Adena). This group developed in isolation from the copper trade, since it broke down with the fall of the Minoan organizers from Crete and Ugarit.

The Algonquian speaking nation went on to adjust to its environment with the new technologies, while those who had become accustomed to agriculture moved south into the richer river valleys in Ohio to become the Adena. The Hudson Bay traders became the James Bay Cree. There is no way to prove these changes did not start before the end of the trade, but the carbon dates correlate, indicating a possible connection.

It is my belief the Wisconsin tribes, known as the Old Copper Complex, took their new technologies and started the Woodland Cultures in that region. They gave up the use of the heavy copper woodworking tools that were probably used for cutting the wood for mining fires, or building, or repairing boats. When they returned to hunting and gathering, they kept the helpful little copper needles, awls, and fishhooks that were light enough to carry. The adaptable little birch bark canoes were probably scaled down models of the larger trade canoes and small ships.

Everyone settled back for 400 years of isolation until about 800 BC, when the Phoenicians had reorganized themselves at Carthage. Then, new contacts were made, and the Hopewell religious traditions began, but, well, that is another book.

Epilog

An Expanded and Updated Look at the Copper Trade

As the first edition of Ancient Mines of Kitchi-Gummi spread out across the country, new information came pouring into my office. The people of New England were especially interested. I began to realize that what I had asked for was happening. The theory was being widened. Now as I prepare to produce the second edition, it is essential to make some new information available. The most important information is that "Old Copper" was probably not a culture as much as it was a sophisticated trade network, which had effects far beyond Lake Superior. The monolithic sun worship sites of New England and the lead mining of Potosi, Wisconsin, were two such seemingly connected activities. The dates were the same, and a connection was obvious

The problem that existed was, "how could I easily integrate new information into the story and not destroy the character of the original book?" Some new Items that could be, were incorporated in the appropriate chapters. The expanded information was handled by putting the following four points in the Epilog. This information is important for two reasons. The first is to answer questions that arose out of the first edition. The second was to provide a format for new evidence that will allow the reader to better understanding the broader context of the trade.

Lake Levels and Time Frames

One question continuously came up. How could Cypriot/ Minoans traders get to the islands of Lake Superior? What about Niagara Falls? This question was natural, since everyone could understand, you needed large boats or ships to carry large, several thousand pound, chunks of copper. The following section should clear this up.

The Ottawa River and Lake Superior

To begin our discussion of this problem, I will start with the oldest "Old Copper" site I have found in the Ottawa River area. The age of this site, like the carbon dates of the mines, will set the stage for some of my later conclusions. The Morrison Island site 6 predates the oldest mine date by a few years. The difference is probably not significant, due to the plus or minus variations in most carbon dates. The carbon dates of this site are "4,700 +/- 150 years before present (2700 BC).

"The Morrison's Island 6 site is located on an island in the Ottawa River in eastern Ontario. It was discovered in 1961 and was excavated in 1961-62. The site contains 18 burials, and 276 copper artifacts including 28 projectile points, a "spud," 39 gorges, 2 knives, two wedges and other objects. Both worked and un-worked copper scraps were common, probably indicating copper manufacture on the site. The site is clearly Archaic in age, and appears·to be affiliated with the Brewerton complex of the Laurentian tradition, defined in New York State. The copper indicates contact with "Old Copper" cultures to the west. A C – 14 date places the site at 4,700 +/- 150 year B. P. Kennedy also provides a review of other copper bearing sites and copper finds in or near eastern Ontario and western Quebec." (49)

The date on this site, 2700 BC, put it 700 years before the beginning of the end of the Glacial Lake Nipissing's maximum water level. This is significant, because the route was used less, after the Ottawa River drainage was sealed off by the glacial uplift northeast of Lake Superior. These changing lake levels are understood by some of those archeologists working in the immediate area as the following quote signifies. Yet I believe many non-local archeologists are less able to grasp its significance.

Copper ore was being extracted north of Lake Superior and distributed via the Ottawa throughout the forbidding Canadian Shield country, down to today's northern New York state. At this time the prehistoric river still drained much of the Great Lakes basin, a legacy of the recent Ice Age (today the Lake Erie route is the sole outlet for the basin). (50)

Many readers of the first edition were also confused by the concept of the changing lake levels. Since understanding this is essential to understanding the facts found in the archeological record, I will try to make this complex problem a little clearer.

During the Glacial Maximum Period (14,000 years ago), ice is believed to have reached a depth of about two miles thick in the area of Hudson Bay. Sometime later, approximately 10,500 years ago, it began to rapidly melt. After the melt, this considerable weight of ice was removed, and the earth's crust began to rebound. This is what is called the "glacial uplift." For a period, the receding glacier blocked drainage to the north and, at the same time, released a lot of water to the south. This created a very complex series of glacial lake levels on the area known as the Great Lakes. In the early stages of the melt, this considerable amount of water flowed east in what is now known as the Ottawa River Basin of Canada. James Stoltman explains this better than most in an article which he calls, *The Archaic Tradition.*

A complex series of geologic processes associated with the expansion and final retreat of glacial ice from Wisconsin caused water levels in the Lake Michigan basin to fluctuate, drastically altering the map of eastern Wisconsin. . . . The ice dam continued its retreat northward after 9000 B.C. and lake levels dropped to successively lower elevations, as lower drainage outlets to the north were uncovered. The decline in lake levels continued in a more or less steady fashion until a low elevation of 230 feet above sea level was attained in the Lake Michigan basin about 7500 B.C. This is referred to as the Chippewa Stage in Lake Michigan. The downward trend in lake levels was reversed shortly after 7500 B.C. when the land along the northern margins of Lake Michigan, rebounding upward as it became relieved of the immense weight of glacial ice that had formerly depressed it, actually rose high enough to again cut off northward drainage. Lake levels thus rose again more or less steadily until about 2300 B.C. when a high water stage, known as the Nipissing Stage, was attained at an elevation of 605 feet above sea level. As the southern lake outlets eroded deeper channels, sometime after 2000 B.C., lake levels dropped again, reaching the 595-foot level by 1200 B.C. in what is referred to as the Algoma Stage. After a standstill, there followed another episode of declining lake levels until about 500 B.C. when the Lake Michigan basin attained its current elevation of 580 feet above sea level, and the lake has remained remarkably stable ever since. (8) p – 216, 217

Although Mr. Stoltman was speaking about the Lake Michigan Basin, the information applies equally as well to Lake Huron and Lake Superior. The drainage to the north he was speaking of was through Lake

Huron's North Channel, up the French River and down the Ottawa River Valley. Lake Superior is only about 20 feet higher than Lake Huron, so the effects on it were basically the same. If I use a few of Stoltman's numbers one can see the difference between the Chippewa and the Nipissing Stages was 375 feet. This means that at the Chippewa Stage, the current high point, where the drainage was cut off, was in excess of 375 feet lower than it is today. This high point was at the old intersection of the French and Ottawa Rivers near Sudbury, Canada.

There is another way to look at it. The elevation drop in the drainage, from a point a few miles out into Lake Michigan just north of the current city of Chicago all the way to the Atlantic Ocean near Quebec City, Canada, was only 230 feet. This distance of approximately 800 miles would equate to an elevation drop of about 3.5 inches per mile. With a high volume of water, this would be a very navigable river. Of course, by 2,000 BC to 1,500 BC, as the uplift was near the Lake Nipissing high-level peak, the Ottawa River section would be getting more difficult to navigate. One can only guess the condition of the river about 700 years earlier, when the people were living on Morrison Island. Obviously, the connection to the lakes still existed.

Cultures to the East

The Ottawa River intersects the St. Lawrence River just north of the New York state line. Lake Champlain and the Hudson River provided access into New York and New England. This location is important due to the effect, caused by the trade, we find on the native cultures of that area.

In the work of James Stoltman and others there is an apparent understanding that the Old Copper artifacts are not limited to the cultures around Lake Superior where it was mined. In the previous quote, Stoltman speaks of *"the Brewerton Complex of the Laurentian Tradition, defined in New York State."* Jeremy Whitlock also indicated the copper went into northern New York state.

Ester and David Braun also reveal the relationships of these Late Archaic people in their work. Note the names, "Lake Forest" and "Laurentian Archaic," are used for the same culture in this area. The Maritime Archaic, however, has distinctive traits.

> *Along the far northeastern coasts, the people developed a way of life closely tied to the sea. Archaeologists now call this way of life "Maritime" Archaic. To the west, in Vermont and New York, the people developed a way of life tied to the interior forests,*

rivers, and lakes called the "Lake Forest" or "Laurentian" Archaic. (51) p – 40

It is the Lake Forest or Laurentian Culture that used or traded copper and old copper artifacts in the Northeast. When one sees the end of the Maritime Archaic in 1500 BC, the question must be asked. "Do they only represent a trade component of the Lake Forest Culture?" I will stop here and go into what I find in New England, but we will return to the problem of these two cultures later.

The New England Connection

The Maritime Archaic way of life began sometime during the Middle Archaic, before 4,000 B.C. (6,000 years ago), and ended shortly after 1,500 B.C. We really do not know why it ended. Coastal sites after 1,500 B.C. contain more shellfish remains, and fewer bones of ocean fish. Also, there are fewer of the heavy woodworking tools than before. From these pieces of evidence, we can guess that fishing and hunting out of the sea, and carving large dugout canoes for ocean travel, became much less important. (51) p - 43

Before I delve into the meaning of the disappearance of the Maritime Archaic way of life from northern New England, we need to study how it presents itself at about 2000 BC. First I will discuss what I found concerning the Red Paint People just after the first edition of my book came out in 2000. I traveled to New England at the request of some of the members of the New England Antiquities Research Association (NEARA).

Maritime Archaic — The Red Paint People

The chemical composition of red ocher is a key piece of information needed to understand these cultural relationships in New England. Archeologists have noticed some burials within the Archaic Period are sprinkled with red ocher. Some seem to have been buried with baskets of red ocher, and others are simply cremated. This use of red ocher is, by no means, a culture-wide phenomenon, but it does go on over a very long period. Another way one could look at this red ocher is maybe it's a burial artifact, more important to the burial of a specific person, than as a broader religious burial practice.

As an example, a great hunter may be buried with his bow, or a great warrior with his battle-axe. In this context, a great spiritual leader may be buried with the blood of Earth Mother, (red ocher), or a rich trader may be buried with a basket of his most richly prized trade goods (red ocher).

To return to the very well written book, *The First Peoples of The Northeast*, by David and Esther Braun, they divide the Late Archaic into three groups. These are the Maritime Archaic, the Lake Forest or Laurentian Forest, and the Atlantic Sea Board. The differences of these three groups, to a very large extent, come from the way they have had to adjust to their environment. It is with this in mind, that I would like you to consider my first point. Two separate cultures could look very similar, if they have had to adjust to the *same* environment, and if they existed in the same time frame. It is within this context that I want you to consider the Maritime Archaic (Red Paint People).

As pointed out earlier, red ocher burials and red ocher paintings exist all across the northeastern USA and in many other parts of the world. They are very prevalent in the Great Lakes region, and on the Laurentian Shield of the USA and Canada.

The First New York Garment Trade

In the beginning of this book, I have made the case for the Cypriot/Minoan traders shipping copper from Lake Superior to the Eastern Mediterranean 4500 years ago. Two of their primary trade items at the time were wool fabrics and garments. A necessary raw material for this trade is dye. It can be assumed these traders would always be on the lookout for new sources of dye. Keep this in mind as I move quickly to the new information.

One NEARA member, in particular, believed she had seen a relationship between the copper mines of New England and the monolithic structures of her area in Vermont. With some skepticism in mind, I traveled there to investigate. The primary reason for skepticism was simple. I had never heard of archaic copper smelting areas being found anywhere in New England. Since the minerals in the mines were copper sulfite and copper sulfate ores, there was no rational way, without smelting, to get the copper to the Mediterranean. However, over the years, I have learned to listen first and judge later because I have limited knowledge of mining chemistry.

What I discovered puts the Red Paint People in a brand new light for me. As I was reading the histories of the copper mines in Orange County, Vermont, I was very surprised to discover they were first used to produce paints and dyes. In fact, Orange County may have gotten its name from its dye production. I was told *Brandon Orange* dye of Brandon, Vermont, is today one of the basic dye color standards worldwide. I also read another of the primary products, of these early mines, was the paint pigment called *Venetian Red*. Even the name implies its use in the Mediterranean area.

Traveling with my friend and two other NEARA people we visited two local copper mines. Upon examination of one of the mines, our party discovered a patch of red ocher along a trail road. It had been a chunk of iron sulfide ore that had been leached by the rain. You could smell the sulfur oxide gas all over the area. Slowly I began to realize the hard chunks of rocky iron oxide ores of Minnesota were really a slightly different chemical formulation than this very soft material before me. People in the northeast did not have to slowly grind the oxide ore into a powder to paint themselves. They could just pick it up. It is no wonder they had enough to carry around in baskets. With this new information, my friend and I examined the second mine site.

We discovered a small spring, coming out of a dead tree that had a root grown down into an ore pocket. This was probably less than 30 years old. The root, now dead, formed a channel in which the spring flowed. The water was clear as it came out of the ground, containing ferric sulfides in solution, but these oxidized on the surface and turned into a muddy mixture of leaves and reddish yellow iron oxide. The resultant patch of red ocher was about six feet by eight feet and one foot deep. It was a fabulous revelation. Red ocher could be just picked up along the streams and springs that drained these bands of decaying ores.

One way to increase and hurry the production of red ocher would be to place the ferric sulfide ores in specially prepared ponds or water sources. Soon nature would make the necessary chemical change. Some evidence of unusual stonework does exist, but as far as I know, no one has been looking for specific sites. A ferric sulfide mine, in the vicinity of a manmade pond, would be the ideal find or proof.

This might have been what the Tinkham culture people were doing with their new temporary camps high up on the ridges in 2000 BC. Had the Minoan traders seen some of these natives painted in red ocher and started securing it as trade goods? Was a red-paint person nothing more than an Algonquin paint merchant, or possibly a local Minoan paint buyer? This is a lot of supposition, but if true, it could answer a lot of questions.

First, why wasn't the red paint used in all burials? Second, why was it so widespread? Like the beaver pelts later, the traders would travel far and wide looking for the product. It could also explain why they might paint the rock walls along their trade routes in red. The native use of red paint would have been ancient also but for different reasons. Their use would be apparent before the trade and after the trade. The natives' desire to create beauty and pleasure would have assured the paint would continue to be used long after the trade stopped. The material also is a preservative when used on paddles or other wooden objects. Maybe they also thought it would preserve the bodies in the burials.

This gave me a lot to think about, as I looked deeper into this eastern Algonquin culture. If there was a trade in fabrics and garments, was there any evidence of wool at this early age? Have their been any discoveries of wool in ancient Algonquin sites? Although it normally would not survive in the moist acid soils of the Northeast there may be a dry cave a little farther south or a limestone association that could preserve some wool fabric. When did the first types of looms show up in North America? These were all question that needed to be answered or at least considered.

Sun Worship and Cosmology in New England

The Stone Chambers

Winter Solstice Stone Chambers: One of the changes that took place during this dynamic period that the professionals call the Late Archaic Period, was the concept of sun worship. The numerous stone chambers, dolmen, cairns, and standing stones found in New England have been a source of controversy since colonial days. When I implied in the first edition of this book, that I believed they were connected to the Cypriot/Minoan miners trade culture, this struck a note of resonance with some New England residents. One of the relationship factors is the sun worship connection. It has been shown on numerous occasions that there is a special orientation of many chambers to the winter solstice or the equinox alignment, far to many to be accidental.

American Stonehenge Site: One such site is called the American Stonehenge. This site, although covered briefly in chapter 7, has much more to offer. It has most of the normal alignments of a complete sun worship sacred site. It has alignments for the North Star, the equinox, plus winter and summer solstice. There also appears to be the apparent use of the four sacred animals of the Algonquin speaking cultures (otter, eagle, bear and turtle). To have both cultures represented is very meaningful. It could mean the sun worship culture was fully integrated into the Algonquin culture by the time the colonist arrived. This would help to explain how the stone chambers could have survived all the centuries. The local natives would have maintained them. One proof of this may be the five-pointed star symbol below.

G - 75 Morning Star Woman Symbol

Algonquian Cosmology: The Abenaki five-pointed star is just such a symbol. When I asked the museum curator what the symbol on the canoe (***pictured left***) meant, he said, *"Morning Star Woman."* *"How long has the symbol been used to represent Morning Star Woman?"* I asked. *"For thousands of years,"* he answered. Yet most people, even today, do not know it is only when you draw up the conjunctions of Venus (the Morning Star) on the background of the Zodiac, that you actually get the five-pointed star symbol.

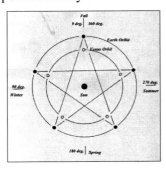

G - 76 Five-Pointed Star Indicated by Mapping the Conjunctions of Venus

Did the early Minoan traders introduce these ideas into the Algonquian speaking people thousands of years ago? Were they integrated with the ancient shamanistic beliefs to become what we call the American sun cultures and/or mound cultures we study today? There is much more to learn about religion and cosmology of the Native American cultures. They are much more complex than we have been led to believe.

The use of the corbelled arch to create the roof in most of these stone chambers has not been satisfactorily been explained. This type of construction was thought to be an invention of the early Minoan culture. It has been, of course, used in Ireland and parts of Western Europe. There is no indication, to my knowledge that the colonial people used it. By the colonial period wood was used as the easiest roof construction material.

The stone chambers, so numerous in New England, are often orientated toward the winter solstice sunrise/sunset or the equinox sunrise/sunset. Sometimes the North Star or other features are included on these sites. The Algonquian religion now appears to include the four dates (the two equinox points and the solstice points) of the sun worshipping traders. These were celebrated as the four earth and sun ceremonies. The five-pointed star became known as (Morning Star Woman), the same goddess that was known as Venus, Diane, and Ishtar in the old-world cultures. The moon, probable always important, also became a Goddess.

The stone chambers were now used to honor the movements of their greater sky beings. They were aware these great sky beings influenced their lives. Their shamanistic past dictated all beings had spirits, so they prayed to the spirits of these great beings. The stone chambers were pointed to the winter solstice sunrise to mark and honor the return of the great sun that was so nearly lost during winter in these northern regions.

This continued through the religious reformations of the Hopewell Period and up until the arrival of the new white men. The religion slowly changed over time, and so the chambers changed also. Most were probably maintained by the family groups that used them, much like the northern Lake Superior Algonquian maintained the red paint sites.

It is obvious to many that various languages have been carved into many of the lintels and interiors of the stone chambers. Carvings are also found in the vicinities on other lithic structures. These languages lead to the Minoans, Celts, Carthaginians, and Greeks.

I believe the alignments of these chambers are solar. This has been well documented in several books. Orientation to the four points of the sun strongly suggests the existence and influence of a sun worshipping trade culture.

Stone Structures and the Mineral Zones

If, as I have indicated, dye and paint were an export from the New England area, then there should be a recognizable correlation, between the mineral zones and the stone structures. These zones are along the ancient fault line in the vicinity of the Connecticut River. On both sides of this fault line, there is substantial evidence of these minerals from Canada to New York. In addition to the iron oxides and iron sulfides listed above the zone also contains copper oxides and sulfides. It has deposits of serpentine (American jade) and steatite (soapstone and graphite), which are all easily carved. The soapstone was used for bowls in this ancient period before pottery was introduced.

A careful analysis of the locations of these structures, along side of the location of minerals known to be used at the time, could be very informative. This should probably be analyzed at the state or local level so map detail would be big enough to reveal a relationship, if one exists.

It is always a good idea for a businessman to stay close to his business. It could also be expected that local merchants who were using air and water to change iron sulfides to iron oxides, would need to be close to their work. The young colonial girl, who found one of the Vermont copper mines, fell into just such a pit of water and iron oxide. She came out an orange color from the dye.

A through study of this early dye trade is too broad to be fully covered here, but it definitely needs further investigation. Someone needs to prepare a general map of the mineralized zones and stone chambers to see if a sound correlation exists.

Stone Bowls and Other Products

A good merchant must always keep aware of potential new products available for trade. He is continually looking for a new product one group holds in little or no value but a second group values very much. The Jade-like greenstone, known as serpentine, may have been such a product.

We have already mentioned paints and dyes, but let's not forget the residents of Cyprus and Crete were also the alchemist (chemist) of their time. They knew how to smelt copper from copper sulfides ores. They were making and selling blue cobalt glass by 1200 BC. They were aware of and using the soft workable stones of serpentine and soapstone. These substitutes for jade and marble may have been in high demand. In fact, these minerals were being mined and used by all three of the Late Archaic peoples described earlier in the book.

I personally observed a small block of this stone found in Vermont. One Greek visitor called it ancient money. It was about 1¼ inches thick, and perhaps 2½ by 4 inches in size. It had Greek letters carved on it. The context was local, but any professional would surely question it, since it could be easily carried.

The early Greeks also used asbestos fiber. In one example, the king used it for table linen and indestructible lamp wicks. This ore is found in large amounts in the mineralized associations of serpentine and steatite in the New England area and farther up into Canada.

Of course the most documented use of these minerals was steatite (soapstone). It was carved into bowls in numerous locations. In recent years a common use for steatite, was for it to be ground into talc.

Evidences of Archaic Mineral use

Kevin Dann, in his book *Traces on the Appalachians: A Natural History of Serpentine in Eastern North America*, describes the use of steatite ore (soapstone) in detail.

> *I've met the ghosts of prehistoric quarrymen farther north, at Ochee Springs quarry in Rhode Island. There, surround by concrete, is a steatite outcrop a few meters wide that bears ovoid scars like the ones seen by W. H. Holmes at the Connecticut Avenue quarries in Washington. D. C. . . .* (another place where bowls were removed)
>
> *The Ochee Springs quarry was discovered in 1878, when workmen on the Horatio Angell "Big Elm Tree Farm" in Johnston, Rhode Island, exposed the earth-covered steatite ledge. It was the first pre-historic soapstone quarry in New England to come to the attention of the emerging professional archaeological community. (52) p-55*

To aid in the comparison of the locations of minerals and stone works, I have included Dann's list of several archaic soapstone sites below. Readers can compare these locations to the known locations of New England stonework.

The Maryland Ceramic and Steatite Company Lands
      (Susquehanna River, PA)
James River Basin, Schyler, VA
Princes Quarry (on the Schuylkill, near Philadelphia, PA)
Westfield, MA
Ragged Mountain Quarry, CT
      (A steatite Quarry and rock shelter)
Horne Hill Quarry (Middlebury, MA.)
      (c. date 730 BC, est. start date, 1700 BC)
The Saxton River (a major tributary of the Connecticut River)
Soapstone shards (in Connecticut River Valley).
Roxbury, Lowell, and Troy VT.
Newfoundland.

Dann also lists serpentine and steatite in other locations, with no mention of archaic use.

Grafton, Bethel, and Rochester, VT
Ottauqueechee River (Woodstock area, Free Stone Hill source)

Distribution of the Soapstone Bowls

We have no information that any of these products actually did go east to the "Old World." In fact, I think it would be interesting to study the distribution of these products further. This section was developed to indicate a motive for Minoan traders and later, Greek and Libyan traders to continue to come to this part of North America (New England), after copper was no longer in demand. The proof that they came can be found in the scattered bits of language they left behind.

In the first part of this book, I ended my history in 1200 BC, when the copper mining became drastically reduced and the so-call, Old Copper Culture laid down its big wood working tools. The local, use shifted to decorative instead of utilitarian. In northern New England and Canada, this end seems to come a little earlier, 1500 BC, but on the lower Hudson and Connecticut Rivers, one of the uses still continued.

The use of the soapstone bowl continued for about five hundred more years, until about 700 BC, when the clay pots replaced it. The Abenaki tribes of northern New England still have a tradition of carving bowls. However, now they are carved from wood, using very specialized knives. I believe the Algonquin, from the lower Hudson and the Lower Connecticut Rivers, continued to trade in this product. Probably residual family members of the once lucrative copper trade continued to utilize these mineralized resource zones, until their culture was overwhelmed by the second trading phase. I call this second phase, the Carthaginian phase, and the archeologists call it the Hopewell Culture.

The Carthaginians may have reopened some of the previous trade in paint, dyes, and serpentine. I really cannot say. However, there is strong evidence they were here doing something. Written evidence is found in numerous locations.

Two New England Cultures

If there were traders as the evidence suggests, and if one culture used the stone chambers of a sun worshiping culture of western Europe, then other evidence of two cultures should exist in New England as it did on Lake Superior. Does such evidence exist? Yes, it does.

Maritime Archaic Culture: Again I would like to refer to the work of the Esther and David Braun. Within the Maritime Archaic culture, there are two very important points to consider. Red ocher (red paint) burial sites are often found in this culture. Second, this group often hunted sea animals and ocean fish, even swordfish.

According to the Brauns the culture shows up about 4000 BC and ends about 1500 BC. The time, 1500 BC, is important in that it marks the end of the drainage of Lake Superior through the Ottawa River. The 4000 BC date is too early for the copper trade, but it could mean North Atlantic trade, possibly in walrus tusks, hides, and oils. These products may have gone back and forth along the edge of the polar ice long before copper became a part of it.

At the end of the Nipissing stage of Lake Superior (1500 BC), the glacial uplift ended the ability of large ships too sail directly into Lake Superior. This could have been the reason for the change in the culture that has been noticed and pointed out by the Brauns.

The Maritime Archaic way of life began sometime during the Middle Archaic, before 4,000 BC (6,000 years ago), ended shortly after 1,500 BC. We really don't know why it ended. Coastal sites after 1,500 BC contain more shellfish remains, and fewer bones of ocean fish. Also, there are fewer of the heavy woodworking tools than before. (51) p 43

This is another one of those strange occurrences where a higher technology appears to be given up. The people did not change; yet, the natives stopped taking ocean fish and animals, and have also quit using the heavy woodworking tools. Presumably the tools were un-necessary to build ships cut firewood for the mines. Would a people actually, for some unknown reason, give up the sea as a way of life? It is my contention they would not. I believe it makes perfect sense that the sea-going element (the Cypriot/Minoan Traders) simply stopped coming when the glacial uplift made the route through the Ottawa River no longer usable. The trades may well have moved south to gain access to the copper up the Mississippi River.

We cannot know for sure the changes described by the Brauns are related to the closing of the Lake Superior drainage through the Ottawa River, but the evidence is intriguing.

New routes developed up the Mississippi River when Lake Michigan began to drained south through Chicago. After 1500 BC these routes became more important. Some trade also came through on the lower St. Lawrence River at Detroit, which was also a drain for this period. Erosion at Detroit would eventually close the drainage at Chicago, but the flat land would still make transportation quite easy. The primary over-winter area, the southern Hudson River and the southern Connecticut River, remained in use. This may have been because of other products available in the mineralized zone of the nearby mountains.

Evidence for a Trade Group in New England

One site that reported copper and red ochre was found in the Indian Museum in Washington, County, Connecticut. A carved double snake, one of which was probably covered with small copper platelets, was one

of the most fascinating items. There are also three carved plummet stones, possibly with B. L. carved in Ogham Script on them. They were found at the gravesite in three baskets of red ocher. Here again, maybe the thought was to preserve these artifacts.

G - 77 Two-Intertwined Snakes, Carved in Graphite

One example of the use of these semi-precious stones, by the copper culture people, was the serpentine atlati weight found in an old copper site near Alpena, Michigan.

New Technologies of the Maritime Archaic

In their work, Esther and David Braun point out several new technologies used by the Maritime Archaic that were, at first, different from the Lake Forest group, but then, eventually, seem to be adopted by the total group.

- Large house with sidewalls different from those of the primary group.
- Use of soapstone bowls for cooking.
- Red paint burials used by only part of the group.
- Use of fishnets.
- Use of fish weirs.

Other Archeologists have pointed out new innovations at the same time period.

- Storage of grains.
- Changing of living habits from riverine sites to scattered highland sites, 2000 BC.
- Return to riverine sites 1200 BC.
- Unusual artifices:

Where are all the bowls? Have large numbers of soapstone bowls been found around the country in ancient sites?

G -78 The plummet, so called fishnet weight, may be for measuring water depth or something else. (Museum in Bar Harbor, Maine)

This plummet was thought to be used as fishnet weight. It was brought up in a fisherman's net in the vicinity of Bar Harbor, Maine. It seems to be a very carefully made artifact just used to weigh down fishnets. These would often be lost. It seems just as likely that it may have been used as a plumb bob or on a line to measure the depth of water on larger boats.

Mitochondrial DNA Proof (the Perfect Witness)

On television each night, we can watch how the new DNA technology is changing criminal prosecution cases in our country. How, we can identify the perpetrator absolutely, with only a small sample of body tissue or fluid. Well, these same technologies are now being used to prove the migration routes, that people used as they spread out across the world. One branch of the human genetic research group is studying what they call, Mitochondrial DNA.

This DNA is only found in the female line and can be used to develop a genetic tree to trace human development over time. It is two complex to present in detail here, but it is one of the best ways to prove the migration routes of populations.

There are five basic founding haplogroups in the Native American population. The first four (A, B, C, and D) support the existing belief, that Native Americans came to North America from Asia. There is some discussion as to when and in how many separate migrations, but there is general agreement on where they came from. However, the fifth haplogroup, "X," has caused a lot of controversy.

The problem is simple. The Native groups that speak Algonquian, especially those of the Chippewa and Ojibwa tribes living in the vicinity of the Great Lakes, have a much larger percentage of the haplogroup X gene than would be expected. In some tribal groups, it is as much as 20 percent. The following statement says it well.

The distribution of haplogroup X is also consistent with a pre-Columbian source. Though presently thought to be most common among speakers of Algonquian languages, haplogroup X, which reaches a frequency of 20% in some Algonquian populations, is geographically widespread throughout North America among groups sharing no close or historic or linguistic ties. . . .

Although haplogroup X is now accepted as a pre-Columbian Native American haplogroup, controversy still surrounds its origin. While the other Native American haplogroups are found in Central East Asia, haplogroup X had not, until quite recently, been identified that far east, occurring in the highest frequencies in Europe and Western Asia. (55) p - 10

This article points out the problem. Many researchers just cannot accept what seems to me to be the obvious. This group was in contact with traders from Europe 3,000 to 4,000 years ago. If the trader also traveled and traded in Central and South America for cocaine and gold, you might expect there to also be some scattered X genes there. ". . . *geographically wide spread . . . no close or historic or linguistic ties*" This quote points to a second theory, a group of traders spread the gene.

Researchers are searching franticly in Asia to find some other way to explain it than having people cross the Atlantic. I, however, find it very rewarding. The more they search, the more they will prove the premise of this book, the ancient Minoans traded in North America from 2500 BC to 1200 BC. In fact, I can now quote a second paper that, for all practical purposes, ties the proof tighter.

"Our sample of haplogroup X consists of a large percentage of shared haplotypes among tribes speaking Chippewa/Ojibwa languages and dialects. The haplogroup X network and

distribution of haplogroup frequency suggest that the populations
with relatively high frequency of haplogroup X experienced an
expansion into the Great Lakes region. This expansion, which
generated a value of θ_s only half that for haplogroup B, must have
occurred much more recently in prehistory than the expansion of
haplogroup B. Archeological, linguistic, and genetic evidence all
strongly support the expansion of Algonquian-speakers from the
Great Lakes region, 2,500-3,000 years BP (Denny 1991; Malhi
et al.2001). Ancient-DNA studies of prehistoric populations from
the Great Lake region demonstrated that this Algonquian
expansion probably occurred 700-3,000 years BP (Schultz et al
2001)." (56)

This quote says two things. Not only does the European haplogroup X exist, but it was brought in at a much later time. The mutation rate for this X gene group is only half that of group B. This means the time of its introduction is only half as long their estimated date for group B. Although the date, 700-3000 years BP, is not a perfect fit, it is not bad. I believe it should be 4500 to 3200 years BP. This is one of the strongest proofs yet of my Cypriot/Minoan traders theory. It also supports that they probably did trade in Central America, South America, and possibly the central United States, as indicated in the earlier quote.

Does this mean two different groups of people were living together in New England? Probably, yes. If so, the amalgam of the two cultures would be in what we now call the Algonquin speaking peoples of the Great Lakes area and New England.

Although they were genetically still 80 percent the same Archaic stock, the religion, technology, language, and lifestyle changes were substantial. One of these changes in religion was the introduction of the elements of sun worshipping cultures.

Conclusions for New England

How does this effect the questions in New England? I can now say thousands of years of trade, between local Algonquian speaking people and the early peoples from Europe and Africa, better explains the existence of these stone chambers and other artifacts then currently held theories. I can also say the motives, and opportunity for such trade seems apparent in the evidence.

The Minoan copper traders probably did live in southern New England and in the vicinity of the mineralized zones. Although copper ore was probably not taken for metal production, the use of copperas and other copper ores may well have been going on. The expensive green and blue paints and dyes, plus pigments such as ferric or iron oxides, may have also been gathered. These are currently used to make the paint pigments, such as yellow, Brandon Orange, and Venetian Red.

Serpentine, and its related ores of soapstone and asbestos, may have been mined for other trade purposes as well as local use. The location of these minerals, in the vicinity of the ancient New England lithic structures, provides the motive for the second group of people theory. Like the copper mines of Lake Superior, they force us to look at the over-simplified native histories the archaeologists are painting for us. It is time these lithic structures are taken seriously for the ancient treasures they are. It is sad to say, but people who do not want answers, will not research the questions. It is quite apparent to me this question is being ignored by some instead of being investigated. I can only guess at the reasons, but one is probably economic. The land values are very high in this part of the country.

Working with and utilizing stone as a raw material became commonplace to these people. Slowly, after 1200 BC, the culture re-adjusted to a primarily subsistence lifestyle, but they were never to be the same as in the old days.

The new culture traded more, and they had different tools. We have named them the woodland culture, because they still lived on the fish, game, and gathered food products, but their life was better. They didn't have to move as much, and winters were more secure because of the storage of food.

Language: The language evidence presented in Chapter 7 needs to be mentioned here. As late as the seventeen hundreds, the Algonquian speaking people were still writing in their ancient Cypriot/Minoan script. There are official land deeds and treaties signed in these scripts. How can this be ignored? Someone should write a book about it. The people of New England deserve no less. The numerous small tribes, of once Algonquian speaking people, have a right to their history. I hope the addition of this little section to my book will help the process along.

Mississippi River — Post Nipissing Sites

In 1500 BC, we find the Maritime Archaic leaving eastern Canada. Some simply went farther west along the St. Lawrence and turned north at Detroit. Yet evidence suggests others might have moved south, all the way down to the Gulf of Mexico and up the Mississippi River.

We know that the mining continued for about three hundred years, after 1500 BC until it ended in 1200 BC. If we use the closing dates of the Ottawa Drainage, we can see that the passage would have been getting more difficult, perhaps as early as 1800 BC, about the time a new trading city became established on the Arkansas River. A city, which had no apparent history, was well into a similar trade as our Maritime Archaic peoples, even to include the sun worship religion. But, before we accept this argument, is there any hard evidence?

The Tobacco and Cocaine Trade

***Mystery of the Cocaine Mummies*:** Hard evidence is always hard to find on cases that are 3500 years old. It was, therefore, very un-expected when a German narcotics examiner uncovered a drug trade during the time of the Egyptian pharaohs. The repercussions of this discovery have not yet been dealt with. Before I discuss this further, I would like to quote the research directly.

In 1999, when I was finishing up the first edition of this book, I had heard of Professor Alice Kehoe's comments on the finding of nicotine and cocaine in the Egyptian mummies, but I was unable to contact her. Without confirmation, I was only able to add one small paragraph on this topic under Miscellaneous Evidence. Since that time, the Internet has brought the knowledge of the world to my fingertips. I now have available the entire transcript of a program carried on a Channel 4 television show from September 8, 1996. The program was called Equinox and the episode was named, *The Mystery of the Cocaine Mummies*.

It was the same story that I had heard about earlier but was unable to locate. It embodies all of the elements of the copper mine story—discovery, publication, and denial by the establishment and finally just ignoring the information. While at the same time they ignored it, it's systematically being challenged by Innuendo and misinformation. Here is the account from the mouths of the actual participants. The statements are taken directly from the transcript of the television interview, a piece of excellent journalism.

Narrator:
"It was in Munich, in 1992, that researchers began a huge project to investigate the contents of mummies. When as part of their studies, they wanted to test for drugs; it was no surprise that they turned to toxicologist Dr Svetla Balabanova for help. As the inventor of groundbreaking new methods for the detection of

*drugs in hair and sweat, she was highly respected in her field. . . .
Dr Balabanova took samples from the mummies, which she
pulverized and dissolved to make a solution. As she'd done
countless times before, samples were put through the <u>GCMS</u>
machine, which can accurately identify substances by determining
their molecular weight. . . ."*

Dr Svetla Balabanova - Institute of Forensic Medicine, Ulm:
" *The first positive results, of course, were a shock for me. I
had not expected to find nicotine and cocaine but that's what
happened. I was absolutely sure it must be a mistake."*

Narrator:
*"Balabanova ran tests again. She sent fresh samples to three
other labs. But the results kept being confirmed. The drugs were
there. So she went ahead and published a paper. The reaction was
a sharp reminder that science is a conservative world."*

Dr Svetle Balabanova - Institute of Forensic Medicine, Ulm:
*"I got a pile of letters that were almost threatening, insulting
letters saying it was nonsense, that I was fantasizing, that it was
impossible, because it was proven that before Columbus these
plants were not found anywhere in the world outside of the
Americas."*

Narrator:
*". . . Balabanova had learned her trade from working for the
police. . . . she had also been taught that a special forensic
technique exists which can show the deceased has consumed a
drug and rule out contamination at the same time.
So, anxious to ensure that her tests on the mummies were
beyond reproach, she used this very technique – it's called <u>the
hair shaft test</u>. Drugs and other substances consumed by humans
get into the hair protein, where they stay for months, or after
death – forever. Hair samples can be washed in alcohol and the
washing solution itself then tested. If the testing solution is clear,
but the hair tests positive, then the drug must be inside the hair
shaft, which means the person consumed it during their lifetime.
It's considered proof against contamination before or after
death." (54) p – 1,2*

The test described has been used in thousands of police cases and is considered 100 percent absolute proof when it's used. There is a second voice we need to hear from concerning this. She is Rosalie David.

Rosalie David – Keeper of Egyptology, Manchester Museum:
"When I was informed that cocaine had been found in Egyptian mummies, I was absolutely astounded. It seemed quite impossible that this should be the case." 954) p -3

Rosalie decided to test the mummies in her own museum, sure that she would find nothing, but that proved not to be the case. Her results had a resounding support of the previous tests.

Rosalie David – Keeper of Egyptology, Manchester Museum:
"We've received results back from the tests on our mummy tissue samples and two of the samples and one hair sample both have evidence of nicotine in them. I'm really very surprised at this." (54) p - 13

Dr. Balabanova's reaction to the above statement could be expected.

Dr Svetla Balabanova – Institute of Forensic Medicine, Ulm:
"The results of the tests on the Manchester mummies have made me very happy after all these years of being accused of false results and contaminated results, so I was delighted to hear nicotine had been found in these mummies, and very, very happy to have this enormous confirmation of my work." (54) p - 14

The narrator also mentioned that Dr. Balabanova had discovered the work of Dr. Michelle Lescot, of the Museum of Natural History in Paris, in which she had discovered tobacco in the mummy of the Egyptian Pharaoh Ramses II. This was explained away by the archaeologists but not quite to the satisfaction of Dr. Lescot. She did a second test from deep inside the mummy and still found tobacco.

Although this was done back in September of 1976, twenty years before the television special, the question had been allowed to languish until Dr. Balabanova brought it up again. Of course, this evidence was not good enough for the archaeologist community at large. One Egyptologist from Oxford University had this to say:

"The idea that Egyptians were traveling to the America is, overall, absurd. I don't know of anyone who is professionally

employed as an Egyptologist, anthropologist or archaeologist who seriously believes in any of these possibilities, and I also don't know anyone who spends time doing research into these areas because they're perceived to be areas with any real meaning for the subjects." (54) p – 1 to 14

In my opinion, the key words here are, "*professionally employed.*" I have found ample evidence that, if any archaeologist were to openly support the idea of early trade, they would be committing professional suicide. Not many people are willing to throw away their career for one intellectual point. I will wrap up the information from this television transcript with Professor Alice Kehoe's comments on the topic. She is an anthropologist from Marquette University with both courage and probably tenure.

"I think there is good evidence that there was both trans-Atlantic and trans-Pacific travel before Columbus. When we try to talk about trans-oceanic contact, people that are standard archaeologist get very, um, skittish, and they want to change the subject or move away. They suddenly see a friend across the room – they don't want to pursue the subject at all. They seem to feel that it's some kind of contagious disease they don't want to touch, or it will bring disaster to them." (54) p - 11

You can get the feeling, by reading the transcript, the Egyptologist just want the concept of early trade with the Americas dropped and forgotten. Of course, the reason for this is quite obvious. Like the photo of the Newberry Tablet, solid forensic evidence is hard to disprove. If it is accepted as real, a lot of old assumptions must be reconsidered. This brings us back to why this information was included in this book.

Ramses II died in 1213 BC, the exact time the mining was coming to a close. If the miners had moved to the Caribbean and the Mississippi River Valley in 1500 BC, when the northern route closed, they would have had access to tobacco on the southeastern shore of the North American Continent. The cocaine would also be available in Central and South America just across the Gulf of Mexico.

Both researchers had come up with the same problem. How could this drug use be if there was no contact between Egypt and the Americas? These plants were only supposed to have been found in the western hemisphere in this distant past. For me, the simplest explanation is the most obvious. There was trade with the Americas, where these plants grew and were used as drugs. The native use of pipes during the Mound

Culture era (1100 BC) was well known. The Carolinas tobacco production is famous in American History, but the cocaine comes from the countries surrounding the Gulf of Mexico. The only culture, that is old enough to be getting established near the end of the mining, yet early enough for the pharaoh Rameses II, is the Olmec. Could this use of cocaine mean our traders did make contact with the natives in Mexico and Central America that long ago? There is much more evidence than drugs, but all we can say here is something must explain the use of these drugs in Egypt 3500 years ago. Now I will refer back to the Mississippi River development.

Oconto Wisconsin Burial Dates

Ancient Lead Mine in Wisconsin: The St. John's mine, in Potosi Wisconsin, had been worked by Indians before white men arrived. A old yellow newspaper article from the 1940's, tacked on the wall, showed a photograph of a perfect little copper pick removed from Indian graves in the vicinity. This well-made little pick looks exactly like one we would have made today. The discovery was made before carbon dating, but the connection needs to be investigated further.

Copper Pick: As this book goes to press, I have not yet found the small pick shown in the news clipping, but I did locate the carbon dates for the Grant county site. An age of 3500 BP was given for this "Osceola" site in Grant County. This is the exact date (1500 BC) we would have expected the traders to move into the Mississippi River Valley.

Poverty Point on the Arkansas River: (Started 1800 BC) One more site that has caused a lot of controversy is Poverty Point. It seemed to pop up from nothing and go back to nothing. This site was described by archaeologists, Little and Van Auken, this way:

"Artifacts recovered at Poverty Point have shown that the Poverty Point People traveled and traded widely. . . . The weights were made of a special hematite found only in Missouri or Southwestern Arkansas. From North Carolina, unique soapstone was brought in to be used for pots. Lake Superior copper, Lake Michigan slate, Ohio flint, and tons of steatite from Georgia and Alabama have been found at Poverty Point."(52) p-76

The earthwork at this site was constructed around 1800 BC. One bird effigy mound was 72 feet high, 640 feet wing-tip to wing-tip, and 710 feet from its head to its tail (53). The access trace is aligned to the rising and setting sun at the Equinox.

> *Archaeology has long accepted a possible Olmec influence at Poverty Point. . . . Some of the artifacts found at Poverty Point closely resemble artifacts found at early Olmec sites along the Gulf Coast of Mexico. Poverty Point's layout has some resemblance to the Olmec sites at La Venta and Corral, both of which were occupied at this time. "It is difficult to avoid concluding that Poverty Point was a product of Olmec influence, and a gateway through which the idea of monumental architecture passed into the Eastern Woodlands. (52) p - 76*

One last thing that was of note at Poverty Point, many clay balls were found, that had been used for cooking. They would either put the heated balls into the water or place them around the food. It is worth noting here, that in Bronze Age Ireland, when people didn't have a big enough pot, they would make a wooden lined pit filled with water and then throw hot rocks into it to cook. Did the cooking with hot rocks exist before this time in the Americas? When and where did this type of cooking develop? These are questions that would be interesting to answer.

Olmec Culture of Mexico

The connection between the Olmec culture and Poverty Point seems to be obvious in light of what we have learned so far. Like so many other groups, the native people in the Olmec homeland would have been influenced by the Minoan traders. In fact, we know one item they were after. Cocaine could have only come from this region.

At least one student of the Olmec culture put it something like this. *"They didn't predate the Classic Maya but were derived from within it."* Was this derived culture simply caused by the influence of trade? The Olmec site at San Lorenzo was first occupied at 1500 BC. This is exactly the right time, if it was discovered when the new southern route was being explored from the Gulf of Mexico and up the Mississippi River.

The evidence found in the story, *The Mystery of the Cocaine Mummies*, is compelling. This implies that some type of Mexican or South American connection did exist. Possibly, the Olmec culture could be the connecting link. I am not trying to stretch the trade farther south, but account for the American products found in Egypt.

One last point, the Olmec culture was supposed to have been the creators of the large stone heads, which look somewhat African. We can tell from the Minoan frescos the traders had both light and dark features. It could well be that these trade fleets had African members. If so, this opens another whole area of discussion, much too large to deal with here, but interesting none the less.

Summery of New Theory

Start of the Woodland cultures: I have studied scores of manuscripts on this subject in the last fifteen years. Each new year, more information would be discovered. To my amazement, this new information nearly always supported the premise of this book. Very often, the new information would just answer questions and fill in holes in my data. More recently, I have come to accept, if the theory is correct and if the work is accurately written, the evidence and information will always fit. This is also the case on the cocaine and DNA work. This seems to be true, even if the author is attempting to disprove this type of migration. I have found many archeologists or other professionals who have done very careful field work. Then, they either ignore some of the exceptions or try to explain them away.

This is quite understandable, since few individuals of any profession have the confidence and/or the means to challenge long held precepts of their profession as a whole. As an outsider, I have no such pressures on me. Hence, like other challengers, I will continue to ask hard questions of the archaeologists. I have learned one other thing. If the researcher ignores or discards all evidence he does not understand, then the truth will probably escape him.

The broad brush I used in this work allowed me to integrate the scattered bits of information from this ancient subject, but it also forced me to treat each piece of information in a very cursory manner. One example of this is the language proof. An entire book could be written on this subject, but it would have to be done by someone much more skilled than I am in language.

After this book, the next logical direction would be to unravel the second phase during the Phoenician era. This is even more complicated, because, by then, there were many more players. For those who would like to start, I would suggest the languages and the DNA are the best places to begin. Do not waste your time trying to prove exchange took place—the evidence is overwhelming. The mound culture artifacts, especially those gathered by the nineteenth century researcher (Soper) and currently held by the Mormon Church, are also a key. This, along with the verbal native histories held by the tribes themselves, would give one an excellent place to start.

Due to the overwhelming historical data and information in this field, it is virtually impossible to cover all aspects thoroughly. Some good books were not used in favor of the more basic hard evidence. Consequently, I am sure in this work you may find occasional errors or omissions. Do not discount the theory or evidence for these minor reasons. Work with the information until you find an acceptable answer. Good luck, as you assimilate the facts and theories presented in this book and allow them to conform to your personal beliefs about what really happened. In the end, we each have a personal view of how history happened. The more accurate these personal histories are, the more we learn and grow. Anyone whose family has been here for more than two hundred years probably has Native American roots of some kind. It is time we write a new more accurate history.

If you have enjoyed this subject matter and are either for or against my theory, please do not stop with this one book. There are many interesting authors out there writing on this and related subjects. In the final analysis, I believe we must dig deeper into this subject, but for me to do so risks the problems of many writers. When you swing such a wide loop, you may catch more errors than truths, and your work will soon be discredited. So I think this is a good place to stop. Thank you for your interest.

Bibliography

Chapter 1

(1) J.W. Foster & J.D. *Whitney, Report on The Geology and Topography of A Portion of The Lake Superior District in The State of Michigan*, Part One (Washington: Printed For The House Of Representives,1850)

(2) Geo. A. West, Copper: *It's Mining and Use by the Aborigines of the Lake Superior Region, Report on the McDonald-Massee Isle Royal Expedition 1928, (*Westport, CONNECTIC.: Greenwood Press, Publishers 1928)

(3) Professor Roy Ward Drier & Octave Joseph Du Temple, *Prehistoric Copper Mining In The Lake Superior Region*, (Calumet, Mich. & Hinsdale, Ill..: Privately by R.W.Drier & O.J.DuTemple)

(4) H. R. Crane and James B. Griffin, "Michigan Radio Carbon Chronology", *Michigan Radio Carbon Date Series, Appendix*, (p-238)

(5) *Michigan Historical Review*., p-48: Sub Ref; Rueben Gold Thwaites, *The Jesuit Relations and Allied Documents*, (Pagent Book Co., New York, NY, 1959, P - 265,276,298.)

(6) James L. Guthrie, "Great Lakes Copper - Still Missing", (*New England Antiquities Research Association Journal*, Volume XXX, No. 3 & 4, Winter/Spring 1996)

(7) Charles Whittlesey, *Ancient Mining On Lake Superior Shore. Smithsonian Contributions To Knowledge,* (155, Published by the Smithsonian Institution, Washington D.C. April, 1863)

Chapter 2

(8) James B. Stoltzman, "The Archaic tradition", (*Wisconsin Archaeology*, Vol.67,1986)

Chapter 3

(9) C. Fred Rydholm, *Superior Heartland*, (Published Privately, Marquette, Mich. 1989)

(10) Barry Fell, "Algonkian Signatures on a Treaty of AD 1681", (*The Epigraphic Society Occasional Papers*, Vol. 13 No. 313)

(11) Evening News, *Old Times in The Sault*, (Sault Ste. Marie., MI, 1923)

(12) Newberry News, November 20,1896, Newberry Michigan.

Chapter 4

(13) Thomas J. Hopkins, *The Hindu Religious Traditions*, (Encino Calif. and Belmont, Calif.: Dickerson Publishing Company, Inc.,1971,)

(14) Barry Fell, *America BC*, (Pocket Books, New York, NY. 1976)

(15) Riane Eisler, *The Chalice & The Blade* (San Francisco, Calif. Harper San Francisco, 1988)

(16) Joseph Judge, Minoans and Mycenaens, Sea Kings of the Agean, *National Geographic*, Vol.153, No. 2 Feb. 1978.

(17) H. C. Crawford, *Summer and the Sumarians*, (Institute of Archaeology, University of London, Cambridge University Press, 1992)

(18) Michael Wood, *In search of the Trojan War*, (pub. by British Broadcasting Corporation; Facts on File, New York, NY, 1987)

(19) Roberta Harris, *The World of the Bible*, (Thames and Hudson Inc., New York, New York, 1995)

(20) James B. Pritchard, *The Ancient Near East*, (Princeton University Press, 1958, 1973)

Chapter 5

(23) Ali-Akbar H.Bushiri, *(Bahrain)* "The Dilmun Civilization - Evidence of the Seals on Trade and Economy", *(The Epigraphic Society, Vol. 9, no 217, Occasional Publications,* June 1981)

(24) George F. Bass, "Oldest Known Shipwreck", *National Geographic*, Vol.172,No.6 Dec. 1987.

(25) Grolier, "The Age of Sail" *(Electronic Publishing Inc.* Ref. Cat.)

(26) Jan Atkinson, *The Viking Ship.*   (Cambridge University Press, Worcester, England, 1987)

(27) Homer, *Odyssey,* (Translated by E. V. Rieu, *Penguin Books, London England, 1946)*

Chapter 6

(28) Ruth Whitehouse and John Wilkins, *The Making Of A Civilization*, (Pub. By Alfred A. Knopf, New York, New York.,1986)

(29) A. B. Tataki, *Corfu*, (Pub. by, Ekdoitke Athenon S. A., Athens, Greece,1979)

(30) William Culican, *The First Merchant Venturers*, (McGraw-Hill Paperbacks, Printed in England, Thames and Hudson London, England, 1966) p - 118.

(31) Richard Harrison, *The Beaker Folk, Copper Age Archaeology In Western Europe*, (Thames and Hudson, London England)

(32) Hawkins, Gerald S., *Stonehenge Decoded*, (Dell publishing Co. NY , 1965)

Chapter 7

(33) Jean-Pierre Mohen, *The World Of Megaliths*, (Published by Facts On File, 1990. New York N. Y. USA)

(34) Peter Harbison, *Pre- Christian Ireland*, (Pub. by Thames and Hudson Ltd. New York, N.Y., 1988)

(35) C. J. Hancock, *The Marriage of Earth and Sky,* (New England Antiquities Research Association Journal. Vol. # xx VlII No. 1 & 2. Dated Sumer and Fall 1993.) p - 10.

(36) J.A. Buckley, *The Cornish Mining Industry*, (Tor Mark Press, Islington Wharf, Penryn,Cornwall.1992)

(37) Stefansson, Vilhjalmur, *Iceland The First American Republic*, (Doubleday, Doran & Company Inc. New York NY, 1936) (p-xv)

(38) Keegan, William F., *Emergent Horticultural Economics of The Eastern Woodlands*, (Center for Archeological Investigations, Southern Illinois University, at Carbondale, Ill. Occasional Paper No. 7)

(39) Leon E. Stover & Bruce Kraig, *Stonehenge, The Indo-European Heritage*, (Nelson Hall Inc. Chicago Ill. 1979)

(21) Paul Budd, *"Seeking the Origins of Bronze Tools"* (British Archaeology, no. 36, July, 1998)

Chapter 8

(40) Thor Conway, *Archeology in North Eastern Ontario*, (Ministry of Cultural recreation, Ontario, Canada, 1981)

(41) Ira Fogel, "The Dispersal of Copper Artifacts in the Late Archaic Period of Prehistoric North America", (*The Wisconsin Archaeologist*, September, 1963)

(48) James H. Kellar, *An Introduction to the Prehistory of Indiana*, Indianapolis Indiana Historical Society, 1982.

Chapter 9

(42) Barry Fell, "Decipherment and Translation of the Newberry Tablet from Northern Michigan", (*The Epigraphic Society, Occasional Publications*, Vol.9, no217, June 1981), p 132 -136.

(43) J. Peter Denny, "Algonquian Connection to Salishan", (*Congres des Algonquinistes, 20e*: Oct. 28-30, 1988: Hull, Quebec), Carlton University, Ottawa, Canada, 1989)

(44) Hooker, J.T., *Reading The Past*, (C.B.F.Walker & John Chadwick; authors), University of California Press, Berkley and Los Angeles, CA, 1990)

(45) D.H. Kelly, Proto - "Tifinogh and Proto - Ogham in the America's", (*The Review of Archaeology*, Vol. 11 No.1, Spring 1990)

(46) George W. Hibbard, "Relics in The Lake Superior Country of A Pre-Historic Race". *Mining Journal Hospital Edition*, (Probable from Marquette Michigan, shortly after the Newberry Article, 11/20/1896.)

(47) M.B. Fretz, Editor publisher, *The Newberry News*, Private Communication to Mr. Kenyon Boyer, Managing Director, Marquette Historical Society, Letter dated, May 12, 1958. (Information from his father the late, Wm. G. Fretz)

Epilog

(49) Kent Bakken, "Annotated bibliography of the Old copper Complex", Syntheses, General Work, Clyde C. Kennedy, Preliminary Report, Morrison Island Site 6, Nat. Museum of Canada, Bulletin no. 106, 1966. Original source, Anthropological Series no 72 Ottawa, Ont. P 100 to 117.

(50) Jeremy Whitlock, "Algonquins to Atoms Along the Ottawa" (Web)

(51) Esther K. and David P. Braun, *The First Peoples of the Northeast*, Moccasin Hill Press, 1996

(52) Kevin Dann, *Traces on the Appalachians*, Rutgers University Press, New Brunswick and London, 1988

(53) Gregory L. Little Ed.D., John Van Auken, and Lora Little, Ed.D., *Mound Builders*, Eagle wing Books, Inc, Memphis, TN, 2001 (Ref. D. Snow, 1976, The archaeology of North america, London: Thames & Hudson.)

(54) Equinox – Channel 4 , September 8, 1996. (Transcript) www.uiowa.edu/~anthro/webcourse/lost/coctrans.htm

(55) Jason A. Eshleman, Ripan S. Malhi, and David Glenn Smith, *Mitochondrial DNA Studies of Native American: Conceptions and Misconceptions of the Population Prehistory of the Americas,* EvolutionaryAnthropology, 12:7-18, 2003

(56) R.S. Malhi, J.A. Eshleman, J.A. Greenburg, D. A. Weiss, B.A Schultz/Shook, F.A. Kaestle, J.G. Lorenz, B.M. Kemp, J. R. Johnson, and D.G. Smith, *"The Structure of Diversity within New World Mitochondrial DNA Haplogroups: Implications for the PreHistory of North America"*, American Journal of Human Genetics, University of Michigan, Ann Arbor, MI, 2002

(57) Sterling & Karlovski P-241 Olmec Dating

Note - References are listed only under the first chapter in which they appear.

About The Author

Roger Jewell was born and raised in Minnesota. He graduated from the University of Minnesota, College of Natural Resources in 1962 with a BS degree in Forestry Management. He completed a 32 year career as a professional forester with the US Forest Service, most of which was in the area of Lake Superior.

He was exposed to the legends and stories of Lake Superior throughout his career. During the last twelve years, before his retirement in 1994, he was the District Ranger at the Sault Ste. Marie Ranger District of the Hiawatha National Forest.

From 1994 to 2000, he was collecting information, photographing and writing about this subject. Since the first edition of this book was published, he has been looking at the broader context of the Minoan traders, especially in the New England area. During the summer of 2003, he and his wife Mary traveled to the Greek Islands of Crete and Santorini, where he examined and photographed many actual Minoan artifacts shown in this book.

Mr. Jewell lives in the Gettysburg, Pennsylvania area. In 2001, Jewell produced a second book called, *Riding The Wild Orb*. It is about the subject of long-term weather extremes on the planet. In it, he calls on his US Forest Service firefighting experience. During the many years he spent in the forest, he developed theories as to what causes the long-term drought cycles he had observed.

The Jewells currently live in the green hills of the South Mountain range southeast of Gettysburg, Pennsylvania.

Both of Jewell's books, *The Ancient Mines of Kitchi-Gummi* and *Riding The Wild Orb,* can be purchased on his web site, (jewellhistories.com).

The Cover

The cover was designed by Mary Jewell, an artist and graphics designer. She received her BA in Art and International Studies. The photo was taken along the beautiful Lake Superior shore in northeastern Minnesota's Arrowhead country. The inserted Cypriot / Minoan Tablet was discovered by two loggers under the roots of a tree near Newberry, Michigan in 1896. It was photographed and the photo was sent to the Smithsonian Institute where it remains today.